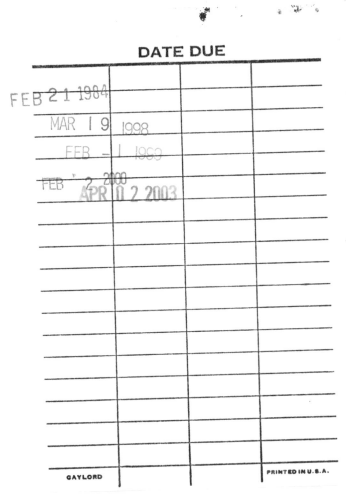

DATE DUE

Poems of
THE HUNDRED NAMES

Poems of
THE HUNDRED NAMES

A SHORT INTRODUCTION TO
CHINESE POETRY
TOGETHER WITH 208 ORIGINAL TRANSLATIONS

BY

HENRY H. HART

[THE TITLE IN IDEOGRAPHS]

The Chinese call themselves by the term
"pai hsing"—the hundred surnames.

GREENWOOD PRESS, PUBLISHERS
NEW YORK   1968

STANFORD UNIVERSITY PRESS, STANFORD, CALIFORNIA

Originally published 1933 as *The Hundred Names*

Copyright 1933, 1938 by the Regents of the University of California
Copyright 1954 by the Board of Trustees of the
Leland Stanford Junior University

Third edition, February, 1954

LIBRARY OF CONGRESS catalogue card number: 68-23295

Printed in the United States of America

FOR MY BELOVED FRIEND
ELSA CAMPBELL McFADDEN

CONTENTS

FOREWORD

A COMPREHENSIVE HISTORY of Chinese poetry is yet to be written, and it seems unlikely to appear until the Western reader can turn from it to a fairly wide range of translated Chinese poems. Of the hundreds of thousands of poems that the Chinese have preserved, scarcely one thousand have been translated into foreign languages, and these translations have been, for the most part, repeated selections from a few of the most renowned T'ang poets. Exquisite lyrics in great numbers remain unvoiced to Western ears. The works of the poetesses have hardly been touched. Those of the pre-T'ang and post-Sung poets have lain virtually unnoticed. The Ming and Ch'ing poets, except a few, have been dismissed with scorn, though many of their quick notations of the heart would reveal the common kinship of spirit that links all the races of men. Fortunately, the number of earnest students of Chinese is increasing, and, with the growing interest in Chinese studies, a background of understanding is being developed, and materials are gradually being accumulated for an adequate survey of the little-explored field of Chinese poetry.

The Chinese themselves possess no complete history of their poetry. Dr. Hu Shih has hardly more than touched upon it in his *Pai Hua Wên Hsüeh Shih (History of Vernacular Literature)*, and only recently have there appeared the first parts of *Chung Kuo Shih Shih (A History of Chinese Poetry)*, by Fêng Yüan Chun and Lu Kan Ju.

The Western nations have made a long beginning of the desired work. It is almost a century since Sir John Francis Davis, President of the East India Company in China, and later Governor of Hong Kong, prepared for the Royal Asiatic Society the first sketch in English of the history of Chinese poetry. This was published in Macao in 1834, under the quaint title, *Poeseos Sinensis Commentarii*. It is not notably instructive. The early Victorian world was much farther removed from China, in human sympathy, than is our own. To the English commentator of that day, the Chinese and their poetry were queer, remote interests, hardly comprehensible. To a Frenchman, presently, they were less distant. The Marquis d'Hervey Saint-Denys published, in 1862, his brilliant *Poésies de l'Epoque des Thang*. Though limited in range, and here and there inaccurate, his book must be considered the first important European-language work on Chinese poetry. Since the appearance of the *Poésies*, much has been done. Legge, Giles, Waley, Ayscough, and Le Gros Clark in English; Imbault-Huart and Soulié de Morant in French; Hauser, Hundhausen, and Forke in German, Chini in Italian, and Alexéev in Russian, have made valuable contributions, and all must be heeded in the preparation of an adequate history.

The following pages seek only to trace the more important developments of Chinese poetry in relation to the historical events which brought them into being. Because biographical notes are available elsewhere, information about the poets has been held to a minimum. An effort has been made to give a serviceable though necessarily incomplete idea of what Chinese lyric poetry is, and of the place it holds, or deserves to hold, in world culture. To this end, the illustrative poems chosen are short, and most of them are here translated for the first time, though a few have appeared previously in German, French, or Italian. To this same end, the verses of many obscure, even anonymous writers, have been included. It is hoped that these verses, summoned from long neglect, will bring something of the life and culture, the charm and beauty, of old China to the younger peoples of the West.

For many suggestions in the revision of my manuscript for publication, I am indebted to Dr. Leon J. Richardson, of the University of California, teacher, counsellor, and friend from my college years. To Mrs. Hattie Hecht Sloss, of San Francisco, whose advice, from rich experience and scholarship, has been invaluable, I wish to express my appreciation. Mr. Pi-Chi Sun, now representative of the Chinese National Government at Bangkok, a Chinese scholar of distinction, has been of great assistance in a careful reëxamination and comparison of the translations with the originals. My thanks are due also to the editors of various periodicals for permission to reprint translations which first appeared in their pages.

Thirty-three poems have been added to those in the original volume entitled *The Hundred Names*. These will be found on pages 214–45.

HENRY H. HART

SAN FRANCISCO
December 19, 1953

THE SPIRIT OF CHINESE POETRY

Lᴵᴷᴱ ᴛʜᴇ ᴘᴏᴇᴛʀʏ of other lands and of all ages, the poetry of China mirrors clearly the thought and spirit of the people. The Chinese conception of the world, and the Chinese interpretation of Nature, of love, and of friendship, are to be found in the lyrics of the Middle Kingdom. As the compositions approach the purely Chinese, and as they express more closely experiences that are peculiarly Chinese, their meaning is apt to elude us, and they therefore tend to lose their hold upon our interest. But it is not so in their interpretation of life—both the life of the spirit and the life of the flesh. As from their ancient past they approach nearer to the European norm, our sympathy and understanding become greater and we are better able to arrive at an appreciation of both the form and the content of the poems. Yet, because these Chinese poets and poetesses do speak to us out of a culture garnered through centuries, some knowledge of the Chinese character, as well as of certain historical events, is necessary to an understanding of that character in verse.

The philosophical background of Chinese culture has always tended to create reflective rather than speculative thinkers. The formalism and traditionalism of the Confucian classics, the interpretation of Confucian philosophy by later writers, the doctrines of filial piety and ancestor worship, the *wu wei* of Tao—all these, blended with the teachings of Buddhism, shaped a mind that inclined to a traditional interpretation of the universe.

This attitude of mind is as dominant in the poets as in the other writers of China. Acceptance rather than questioning, resignation rather than rebellion, is the normal Chinese attitude. A Tu Fu may revolt at the idea of war, and of men killing their fellow-men in battle, but he trumpets forth no summons to do away with the evil. Chinese poets sing of war and its glories, but no Chinese has ever written a "Marseillaise." Perhaps half of the poems in every Chinese anthology are on parting and its pain; but where is the cry to abolish the political system which imposed the forced separation? Even in the beautiful love-lyrics of the poetesses, amid all the heartaches of farewell, and in spite of grief over infidelity or desertion, we find no voice of protest crying out against the man-made standards which permitted such hateful things to be.

East is East, and West is West. There is truth in that familiar line. Certain human relations are so much a part of our Occidental experience and background that we do not realize that they are not necessarily universal.

The greatest of these is the love between man and woman. To the Western peoples it is a mysterious thing, one of the ends and aims of existence, and the greatest preoccupation of the Western poet. To him, woman is the embodiment of the ideal; man is created but to attain and possess her, if he prove himself worthy. The poet revels in picturing himself as that lover, and does not hesitate to bare his heart and soul, to sigh and to pray, to weep and to plead, that all the world may know his passion. We of the West do not find this unmanly—if it is well done.

[5]

To the Chinese, the relation is a commonplace. Perhaps the Chinese betrothal and marriage system is the cause of this attitude—unless, perchance, it is the result of it. Certain it is that, among almost all Chinese, women have always been regarded as the weaker vessels, created to satisfy the needs of the body, to be the mothers of the race and the handmaidens of the household, in all things subservient to their lords and masters. Under this interpretation of the relation between man and woman, love perforce tends to take a subordinate, even unimportant place in Chinese poetry. There are exceptions. Some Chinese poets—not many—have sung beautiful songs of romantic and marital love. The poetesses, as might be expected, have gone much farther; many of their verses approach, in emotional fervor, the lyrics and love-songs of the Western world.

Among the Chinese, friendship between men largely occupies the place in life which love fills for us. We seek sympathy and understanding, companionship and solace, in our wives and sweethearts; the Chinese turn first to their friends. Aside from the hetærae, they can look only to them for intellectual companionship, because, the courtesan excepted, education has been the exclusive privilege of the man. The sharing of life's joys and sorrows with a friend is the burden of many a Chinese poem, and idealized friendship has inspired some of the finest lyrics in the language.

The theme of friendship has appeared also in another guise. China's governmental system, which forced state servants to travel frequently and far from home, sometimes for years, separated close friends and severed bonds of lifelong devotion and affection. Small wonder is it, then, that perhaps half of the tens of thousands of Chinese poems yet preserved sing of friendship and tell of the heartaches of parting, the pleasures and joys of reunion.

More than to any other people, except only the Japanese, perhaps, Nature has been ever present to the Chinese. From the beginning, the Chinese people have lived close to the soil. Nature in her alternating seasons, in her changeable and varying moods, is unceasingly immanent in Chinese life. Little in the life-history of plants or animals has escaped them. Surely, none but the keenest observers of insect life studied the life-cycle of the silkworm closely enough to gain its priceless secrets for mankind; and this was done at least two thousand years ago.

This closeness to Nature, this quick sympathy with all her moods, is evident at every turn in Chinese verse. The coming of the plum blossoms in spring, their scattering fall, the warmth and sunshine of summer in the country, the whispering of the bamboos, the beauty of the lotus pools, the moon and its reminder of home, the song of the brook, the melancholy of autumn, the dripping of chilly rain in the pines, the country white-mantled in winter—all these are often-used refrains in the songs of the sons of Han, from Confucius to the Republican revolution. We see the oriole on the swaying branch, the wild goose winging his flight through the gloomy autumn sky; we hear the call of the cricket from the forest, the bark of the dog welcoming his tired master home at sunset, and the crowing of the cock at early dawn. We feel the sadness of an autumn sunset or the joy of a dewy morning in spring. They are pictured so often and so vividly that we, too, feel them as symbolic of human love and joy and suffering. To appreciate the passionate love of the Chinese for Nature is to understand their poetry, and, through their poetry, to glimpse their souls.

In the commonplaces of life, inherited folk-tales and folk-ways, conventions and inhibitions which surround man from the day of his birth until the day of his death, there is a wide divergence between the Chinese and the Western world. Their stars have different names, their constellations different legends. Their mythology of world forces and natural phenomena is poles apart from ours. To us the moon spells romance; to the Chinese it means loneliness and nostalgia. We have a "man in the moon"; the Chinese see in it a woman, or a hare pounding the elixir of life in a mortar. These examples out of many will suffice to indicate how different is the world that unfolds to the Chinese mind.

But these divergences from our ways and traditional views should not prevent our appreciating the poets of the Orient. We even sympathize with their emotional experience, so much does genius transcend differences. As we read their verse, we realize, when we have cast aside prejudice and taken on understanding, that humanity is everywhere fundamentally the same. The same blood-stream courses through Chinese veins as through ours. The same depths of emotion are stirred by the same causes, love is love, sorrow is sorrow, and joy is joy, whether in the land of the Dragon or in the countries far beyond the Western Sea.

THE HISTORY OF CHINESE POETRY

WE OF THE WESTERN WORLD seldom realize how many more people have lived under the Chinese cultural tradition than have lived under that of Europe. Their tradition is at least one thousand years older than our own, even though we trace our heritage back to the Greece of Homer and the Hebraism of Moses. Not only is the cultural tradition of the Chinese older than ours, but, unlike ours, diversified as it has been by the successive waves of invasion and foreign influence which have swept over Europe, theirs is an unbroken tradition of a largely homogeneous people.

The Chinese, within historic time, have dwelt in the same place; there their genius and culture have taken root and given forth bud, blossom, and fruit. China, in the four thousand years of its historical existence, has been invaded and conquered time and again by Tartar, Mongol, and Manchu; but, though these have imposed short-lived dynasties on the people of Han, their cultural influence has been very slight. China, never failing to assimilate its invaders and conquerors, has gone on its way placidly and immutably, culturally intact. The tradition, from its origins until the revolution of 1911, has been unbroken. This continuity is evident in Chinese poetry at every turn, in both form and content.

The *Weltanschauung* of a Chinese of the nineteenth century was much nearer that of his Han ancestors of two thousand years ago than was that of the nineteenth-century European to the world conception of Chaucer. The language of the

Book of Odes, reputed to have been written more than two thousand five hundred years ago, is more comprehensible to the modern Chinese than is the language of the *Canterbury Tales* to us. In fact, the writings of Confucius still serve as the model of literary perfection for the Chinese.

Early tradition traces the beginnings of Chinese song to at least 2000 B.C., but this claim is as yet without verifiable basis. Chinese authors assert that the first poem of the present collection (see p. 37) was written about 2300 B.C. If so, it is an interesting indication of the unchanging character of the Chinese. The farmer of the "The Hundred Names" is the farmer of *The Good Earth,* and his song is as expressive of the attitude of mind of the Chinese farmer to-day as of the attitude of mind of his ancestors forty centuries ago.

Passing over the folk-songs and occasional poems of the misty, uncertain period of early Chinese history, we are on firmer ground when we reach the *Shih Ching* or *Book of Odes,* which, according to tradition, was collected and edited by Confucius in the fifth century B.C., that glorious period which gave to mankind, both East and West, the most brilliant group of thinkers and teachers that the world has ever had at any one time.

The *Book of Odes* was an anthology of three hundred and five poems and ballads, chosen by Confucius from an older collection of more than three thousand, which had been gathered at various times and in various places throughout the Empire. Confucius considered the *Odes* so important that he told his son he would be unfit for the society of intellectual men until he knew them by heart.

The *Odes* have been annotated and translated by Couvreur into French, and by Legge into English, but there is room for a finer metrical translation more sensitive to the rhythm and word-values of the original. Few of these lyrics—perhaps fifty or sixty—are of common interest. They give an illuminating glimpse of the culture of ancient China, rites and ceremonies in public life, and manners and customs in private life.

The next famous name in Chinese poetical history is that of Ch'ü Yüan (*ca.* 330 B.C.), who wrote a long, rambling poem, the "Li Sao," or "Falling into Trouble," an allegory of politics inextricably tangled with love. Ch'ü Yüan is one of those shadowy personalities that appear often in the annals of Chinese literature. The legends of his life and death are still told to Chinese children; and the annual Dragon Boat Festival, still celebrated in many parts of China, commemorates his suicide and the search for his body. Many efforts have been made to translate the "Li Sao," which seldom makes a strong appeal to the foreign reader.*

The feudal system of the Chous fell under the assaults of the Kingdom of Ch'in, that short-lived but powerful dynasty which has given to China its name and its greatest monument, the Great Wall. Again the land was torn and ravaged by internal strife and anarchy, until Kao Tsu, the first of the Han rulers, established his capital at Hsi An Fu, and China settled down to four hundred years of peace. Under the influence of the Confucian doctrine, the authority of the throne gradually supplanted that of the feudal nobles, and the

* See, especially, the annotated translation, with the Chinese text, in the "Li Sao" by Lim Boon Keng, President of the University of Amoy.

Imperial court became the center of the national life. Under the patronage of the emperors, some of whom were themselves talented poets, the irregular verse-forms of the classics were polished and perfected. New vigor and imagination, a greater richness of imagery, characterize the poems of this era.

Mei Shêng (d. 140 B.C.) has been called the father of modern Chinese poetry. To him is attributed the five-character line, one of the two dominant verse-forms in use since his day.

Liu Hêng (*ca.* 180 B.C.), Liu Ch'ê (*ca.* 156 B.C.), and Wu Ti (157–87 B.C.), three occupants of the Imperial throne, were devoted to poetry. The lament of Wu Ti over the death of his concubine Li Fu Jên (see p. 42) is one of the most pathetic lyrics in the language. The eager ear listening for the sound of a footstep that has ceased forever, the gloom and desolation of the deserted bedchamber, the dull ache and pain of the heart which no anodyne can ease, the emptiness and vanity of life—all compressed into thirty characters—give an unforgettable picture of grief over a lost one.

The pressure of the barbarians on the frontiers, which the early Han emperors had successfully resisted, gradually grew so strong that the capital was moved from Hsi An to Lo Yang. Feeble emperors were unable to control their mutinous generals, and finally one of the latter, Ts'ao Ts'ao, dethroned the emperor in 220 A.D., and the once mighty dynasty of the Hans came to a miserable end.

The centuries of Chinese history between the fall of the house of Han and the accession to the throne of Kao Tsu, the first of the T'ang emperors, were turbulent and war-torn. Civil war and Tartar invasions split the country into what are called the Northern and Southern courts. There was little leisure for the arts of peace; besides, the Imperial patronage was lacking. Yet, in spite of the stress and storm that racked the Empire until the iron hand of the T'ang subdued it, a fair amount of good work was produced by the poets. T'ao Ch'ien (365–427 A.D.) and Pao Chao (d. 466 A.D.) have been translated in part, but many of the poems of lesser-known writers may be found more interesting.

Yüan Ti, better known as Hsiao I (508–554 A.D.), fourth emperor of the Liang dynasty, obtained the throne by murdering his brother. At the end of a stormy reign, and after burning the Imperial library, he was captured by the Western Wei, who put him to death. Warrior, fratricide, emperor, patron of the arts, he was also a poet. He was the strange anomaly—a tyrant and an artist—which occurs more than once in Chinese history. His "Confession" (see p. 75) might, *mutatis mutandis,* have been written in America to-day. In this poem, as in "A Letter," by Chang Chi (see p. 86), is a strangely profound understanding of the soul of woman—an understanding possessed by many Chinese poets.

Tzu Yeh, a poetess of the Chin dynasty, is considered by many critics to have been the originator of the romantic lyric. Beautiful and well known are the one hundred and fifty of her poems which have survived her, but little is known of their author. Even the dates of her birth and death are a mystery. The only information available is the following short note, prefacing her poems in the *Ch'üan Chin Shih:*

In the collections of Chin, Sui, and Chi lyrics, and in the *T'ang History of Music,* mention is made of the songs of Tzu Yeh. We learn from a note in the *Lyrics of the Chin Dynasty* that there was a woman named Tzu Yeh, who created a type of song with a mournful refrain. These were adaptations of old folk-songs. In the Han collection (the *Lo Fu*) we learn that they were called *Tzu Yeh's Songs of the Four Seasons.*

Further than this brief notice and a similar paragraph in the *Tzu Yüan,* nothing is known of this gifted woman. But her exquisite lyrics are a lasting monument to her memory.

Even in translation, shorn of the delight that only the ideograph can bring to mind and eye, these lyrics, each twenty characters in length, convey the life that was ancient China. Dead beauties rise from their graves and live again, moving in a ghostly world of stiff brocades, high-walled gardens, plum blossoms, and courtly manners. The faint odor of incense is about us, and the soft breezes waft to us across the centuries the sweet scent of blossom-time, the tinkle of lutes, and the piping of jade flutes. Brave men ride away to war, and ivory-tinted, moth-eyebrowed wives and sweethearts wave their last farewell through a mist of tears. The lover's heart aches for his mistress far away, and his sighs trouble the moonlit night. How brave they all seem, these people of a world that now is dust! To how many of us

> The brilliant moonlit night
> Seems never-ending,
> And the blessed, longed-for sleep
> Will never come!

How often do we

> ... lie awake, alone,
> And eat the bitter herb
> Of heartbreak and neglect!

[14]

She must have loved, for her songs are full of the sweet sorrow of love and of the tenderness and gentleness that only love can know. So Tzu Yeh, the unknown, neglected poetess of the Chins, looked out upon the world and its romance and heartache, and, taking up her brush in sympathy and in understanding, wrote her songs. Unknown, a name without a history, she has left behind her songs so vital, so human, so full of grace and gentleness, that they sing for us as sweet a melody as they did for the courtiers of the land of Chin, seventeen hundred years ago.

The Sui dynasty, though it lasted less than forty years (581–619 A.D.) and embraced the reigns of but four sovereigns, had the most important line of emperors between the fall of the Hans and the rise of the T'angs. It was a period of feverish activity. The construction of the Grand Canal, linking the great river systems of China, was undertaken. Military expeditions were sent against neighboring states. Lo Yang, the capital, was rebuilt. Buddhism, which had been slowly gaining headway since its introduction, about 67 A.D., began to show its influence on the Chinese social order, and brought new ideas, both philosophical and religious, into Chinese poetry. In spite of the anarchy and strife of these few years, poetry flourished remarkably under the Imperial patronage. The most famous writer of the Sui dynasty, Hsieh Tao Hêng, was put to death by the emperor Yang Ti, constructor of the Grand Canal, because he wrote better verse than his Imperial master—a folly not unknown in other courts.

The T'ang dynasty, like the Han, has left its name indelibly stamped on the memory of the Chinese people. To this day the Southern Chinese speak of themselves as *t'ang yan*, or "Men of T'ang." The most brilliant in intellectual achievement of all the dynasties of China, it fostered an Augustan Age of Chinese literature. Every condition requisite for the rich flowering of the poetic genius was present; peace and prosperity at home, victory abroad, a great literary tradition, a language grown rich in epithet and metaphor, all united to give birth to a glorious era of poetry.

Under the generous patronage of the emperors, many of whom were poets themselves, the most brilliant writers of the Middle Kingdom gathered at Chang An, the capital. With the technique of poetry perfected, its rules and methods definitely established, the T'ang poets poured forth their songs in bewildering beauty. As a Chinese critic has written: "The tree of poetry took root with the *Odes,* its leaves sprouted in abundance under the Han and the Wei, but it was given to the T'angs to see its flowers and taste of its fruits." This perfection of form and thought was never surpassed by later generations, and T'ang poems are still the models for all Chinese writers.

A large volume would be necessary for a mere mention of the poets of this period. Wang Wei, Tsu Hao, Li Po, Chang Chien, Tu Fu, Po Chü I, Wei Ying Wu—these and the names of many other glorious singers come at once to mind.*
One marvels at the beauty and simplicity of form, the clarity

* Material for the study of some of the great poets of this era is abundant. Li Po, Tu Fu, and Po Chü I are represented in most anthologies of Asiatic poetry. Others, like Wang Wei, great physician, painter, and poet, of whom it was said that his poems were pictures in words, his pictures poems on silk, are less known than they deserve to be.

of language, the richness of the vocabulary. The content of the poems is no less rich and varied. Poems of love and friendship, of philosophy and religion, rollicking songs of the wine-bibber, laments for the dead, songs of farewell and welcome, epigrams, occasional pieces, ballads, pleas for peace, exaltation of war, all pour forth in endless abundance from this seemingly inexhaustible spring of T'ang poetry. Yet these poets, even Li Po, borrowed heavily from the writers of former generations. In many of the finest T'ang poems we find the devices and ideas of preceding eras. The lesser poets sought to hide their paucity of ideas behind refinements of form and an ever growing wealth of classical allusion. These two tendencies mark the beginning of the decadence which was later to undermine and destroy classic poetry.

The T'ang empire, like its predecessors, was trodden out in a welter of blood. Fifty years of civil war followed on the heels of revolt. Finally, a new dynasty, that of the Sungs, again brought the Empire under strong central control. But even the Sungs were always at war. The Tartar hordes of the north, hungry for land and plunder and ease, had begun to besiege the Empire with an ever increasing pressure which finally, after four hundred years of struggle, was to result in the ascent of the Mongol dynasty to the Dragon throne. It was war to the death between the civilized, highly cultured Empire and the barbarians.

Yet, in spite of these external troubles, the Chinese were able not only to maintain their civilization, but also to develop their commerce, institute many reforms, and produce great artists, poets, and philosophers. The poets of the new empire of the Sungs, however, had lost something of the divine fire that had burned so brightly down the centuries. Form and formalism gradually took the place of thought and originality. Decay had set in. Convention restricted the play of the imagination. Mere metrical cleverness was valued more than the thought-content of the poem. Rhyming dictionaries and form-books made poetry a pastime of the clever rather than the spontaneous outpouring of inspired souls. The great names of this period are Wang An Shih, Su Tung P'o, and Ou Yang Hsiu. Of these, Su Tung P'o is the best known, though the lyrics of Wang An Shih are nearest to those of the T'ang writers in spirit and form.

The feeble empire of the Sungs was no match for the vigorous, steppe-dwelling hordes of Mongols, and, after repeated assaults, the tide of Mongol conquest swept over the North. The Sungs fled southward to Hangchow, which remained their capital until 1276, when the Mongols captured it. With the fall of Hangchow the great Sung empire came to an end.

The Yüan, or "Everlasting" dynasty, was of short duration. The Mongols, invincible in war, could not withstand the enervating influences of civilized life. Their sudden transformation into city dwellers, the abandonment of their wild, simple, desert life for the complex life of the court, soon demoralized and enfeebled them. In little more than a hundred years they had given fifteen emperors to China, and had vanished into the desert whence they had come. Under their sway, a fair amount of mediocre poetry, mostly warlike, was written, possessing none of the old fire or spirit. In 1787 the Emperor Ch'ien Lung gathered together eight volumes of Yüan poetry, but there is little of it which repays the labor of translation.

Great soldiers, the Mongols were inefficient administrators. As their grip on the government weakened, rebellion became rife throughout the Empire. Finally, under the leadership of Chu Yüan Chang, a Buddhist monk, the Chinese drove out the degenerate descendants of Genghis Khan and established their own leader in Nanking as Hung Wu, first of the Ming dynasty.

Throughout the three hundred years of Ming rule, literature was protected and encouraged. A great deal of verse was produced, but few great poems. As if to compensate for a lack of inspiration in the men poets, the women of the Mings wrote many lovely lyrics. Hsü Ching Fan, Ku Shih, P'an Shih, and other dainty ladies of the court have left exquisite pictures in verse, as well as numerous love-songs and laments, without which the world would be the poorer.

By the second quarter of the seventeenth century the glory of the Mings was waning fast. Misgovernment, and the ascendancy of eunuchs in state affairs, inevitably brought in their train discontent, brigandage, and rebellion. Peking fell, and the Manchus, who had been summoned to aid in suppressing the revolt, seized the throne. In 1644 they imposed the "pigtail" on the Chinese; and they ruled the land until the advent of the Republic in 1912.

In the two hundred and fifty years of Manchu rule, a vast amount of poetry was written. The emperors wrote much, Ch'ien Lung's verses alone numbering more than thirty-three thousand, nine hundred separate compositions. Correct

[19]

enough in form, they are all lifeless, and hardly worth translating. The most popular poet of the eighteenth century was
Yüan Mei (1715-1797). In his versatility and brilliance he
seems to be an echo of the glorious epoch of the T'angs. But
almost all the poetry of the Ch'ing dynasty is merely stiff,
artificial verse, devoid of beauty in form or in thought. The
exceptions, as in the Ming era, are from the hands of the
women, many of whom wrote delightful lyrics.

With the revolution of 1911 came an influx of foreign ideas,
the study of foreign models, and the efforts of young poets
to substitute the vernacular for the classic language in their
verse. But these fascinating subjects have no place here.

Another word about the older times. No sketch of Chinese
poetry, however brief, would be complete without mention
of the women who have given to their race some of its love-
liest lyrics. Most of these women are only names. All other
record of them has vanished—except the poetic legacy of
beauty. Yet there is no period in Chinese literary history without its poetesses. Many of the *Odes,* even, must have been
written by women; the feminine spirit that pervades them is
unmistakable. (See p. 39.)

That the Chinese have always appreciated their women
authors is evidenced in the anthologies, even in those which
have come down from the earliest times. From Tzu Yeh to
Hsi P'ei Lan, Chinese women have written imperishable
songs. In some strange way they have drawn more intimate
pictures of family life, and exercised a deeper insight into the
Chinese heart, than have even the greatest of the poets.
Which of the men, even the most illustrious, would reveal

himself as Tzu Yeh has in "Through Your Window"? (See p. 54.) "Waiting," by Ts'ui Ying Ying (see p. 121) is as old as the world of lovers, and the hedonism of "Wise Age to Youth" (see p. 122) is of the same temper as that of Epicurus —or of the post-war generation in the West. The "Drums" (see p. 47) is more than Chinese, it is the heartache of any agonized lover "when love is done." The Chinese may hide their emotions behind a mask, and repress their joy and sorrow and suffering in order that none may see or know, but their women poets give lightning-clear glimpses into the innermost depths of souls. And how like our own they are, the hearts and souls of these women of another world, another time, and another race!

The happiness of "Joy" (see p. 65), when spring and love return together, the pride and artlessness of the maid who worshiped at the shrine of Hu Chiu Shan (see p. 156), "The Keepsake" (see p. 161), "The Awakening of Spring" (see p. 163), and "Alone" (see p. 99) are songs that are true the world over. Their language is Chinese, but their voice is the universal voice of womankind.

As the poetess thanked Heaven for her "shrine among the trees" (see p. 166), so may we be thankful for these exquisite lyrics, to add to the store—ever too small to satisfy our cravings—of those songs to which our hearts turn, as did Mêng Shu Ch'ing's, when we, too, are "weary of this sad world, and of man's turmoil and strife."

The grief of a daughter for her mother (see p. 176), the shadowland of dreams (see p. 178), memories which so often bring "fresh pain to the wounds we had thought long healed," the quaint conceit of "The Spring Wind" (see p. 66), the love of a wife for' her husband, the world at eventide (see p. 135)—all are universal experiences. We rejoice in the flute lessons (see p. 208) and the mother's pride in her son, we are anxious with the housewife when a guest comes unexpectedly for dinner (see p. 209), and our heart aches with the "Mother" (see p. 207) who sits, dry-eyed and speechless, by the body of her dead child.

These women of China offer something so akin to our own emotions and responses that we gladly receive it as ours, too. It is for this reason that the translator has ventured to include so many of their poems in the present collection.

THE TECHNIQUE OF CHINESE POETRY

RHETORICAL DEVICES and figures of speech are used by the Chinese with greater restraint than by us. A people more concrete in their thought and language than ourselves, their similes and metaphors are simpler, and employed more sparingly than those used in the languages of the West. In the succession of centuries these figures finally became so stereotyped that they rival in artificiality our commonest *clichés*. At first an ornament to the poem and a joy to the reader, classical allusion and epithet became so numerous and obscure as to require concordances and encyclopedias for their elucidation. With decreasing fertility of imagination and increasing inflexibility of form, these allusions became so burdensome that they destroyed the joy of reading poetry. Employed by the poetaster to display his erudition, their niceties and studied obscurities finally cramped, crushed, and destroyed the Chinese poetical genius.

The most effective device employed in Chinese verse is parallelism. Strangely enough, it was the favorite and most telling rhetorical device of another Asiatic people, the Hebrew. Parallelism is a symmetry of arrangement, having "a marked correspondence and equality in the construction of the lines—such as noun answering to noun, verb to verb."*

Hebrew poems are replete with parallels. Much of the beauty of Biblical verse is in the majestic, cadenced music of parallel verses. One has but to read aloud the Twenty-third

* Cranmer-Byng, *A Feast of Lanterns.*

Psalm, or some passage from the prophets, to realize the power of this simple device. "Like the swing of a pendulum to and fro, like the tramp of an army marching in step, the versification of the Bible moves with a rhythm of parallel lines."*

The Chinese have used this scheme with like result; the lines pulse and beat with a measured cadence that intensifies the emotion and makes more vivid the picture which the poet would convey to his reader's consciousness. Sir John Davis has given numerous examples of this parallelism, of which the following illustrates the principle:

> The fine flower unblown exhales no sweets.
> The fair gem unpolished emits no radiance.
> Were it not that once the cold penetrated its stem,
> How could the plum blossom emit such fragrance?

Another favorite scheme of the poets, one which ever delights, is the "short stop," usually a poem of four lines. Just enough is written to suggest to the mind a train of thought. Then the poet "stops short," leaving the reader to develop the thought further in his own way. It is a form of verse as old as the Han dynasty, and endless in variations.

Chinese poetry, however, is not primarily written to be read aloud. Its beauties of composition are for the eye, not the ear, to enjoy.

In the first place, five- or seven-syllable verses, when read aloud, become monotonous and soon cease to give pleasure. Secondly, with changes in pronunciation since the poems were written, rhymes and assonances have tended to change,

* Moulton, *The Literary Study of the Bible.*

[24]

and much of the original sound-rhythm is lost. Thirdly, when written in *wên li,* the classical language, and in classical style, the poem would not be understood by many listeners, not even by speakers of *kuan hua,* the official language of China.

But reading with the eye alone, rather than with both eye and ear, has its compensations. The ideographs bring to the student a wealth of imagery, a world of meaning in form and color, and an interpretation which can never be fully conveyed in a translation. The pictures embodied in the ideographs more than compensate for the extreme terseness and compactness of the grammatical structure of the verse. These pictures have their own connotation in addition to the word-idea which they represent. For example, the ideograph *an* is defined by Giles as *still, quiet, rest, peace.* The ideograph pictures a woman under a roof. *Hao* is defined as *good;* the ideograph is the picture of a woman and child. *Ming* is *bright;* the picture is of the sun and moon in conjunction. *Nan, male,* is a field plus the sign for strength, and *nü, woman,* is a person with a pack on her back. Let these examples suffice to indicate the implications of the ideographs. They embody Chinese historical, social, and personal experience. Each character, when analyzed, will be found to contain a rich connotation, and, carefully chosen as they are by the poet, they make a poem more than the series of ideas or emotions which the words express when taken without further visual or mental interpretation.

Thus each poem may be likened to a Chinese painting, which, slowly unrolled, brings into view a succession of exquisitely drawn pictures, each conveying a vision of beauty or a dream-tale. One enjoys getting the simple meaning of the verse, but a more subtle and lasting pleasure arises from contemplating the profound meaning, with its shades of difference and pleasant excursions, conveyed by the ideographs. The study of the ideographs has been a labor of love with the Chinese for two thousand years, ever since Hsü Shên, in the first century A.D., wrote his famous *Shuo Wên,* the first etymological dictionary. This dictionary is but now attracting the attention of Western scholars.

In the poetry of all languages, use is made of certain elements inherent in human speech. The most important of these are rhythm and rhyme. In European languages, rhythmical effects are obtained by a succession of certain syllable groups, or by the stress-accent. Each language uses those elements which are most characteristic of it; for example, Latin and Greek had alternation of long and short syllables, and English rhythm is produced by the use of stress-accent. Rhyme, the correspondence of terminal sounds in verses, arranged in a predetermined manner, is the second familiar element in the composition of poetry.

The elements employed by the Chinese in their early poetry were, first, the natural rhythm of the language produced by lines of varying length, and, secondly, rhyme. According to Waley,* the *ku shih,* or poetry in the "ancient style," employed thirty-four rhymes, though many of them were merely assonances.

With the growth and development of Chinese poetry a fuller, stricter, and more complicated rhyme-system gradually

* *Notes on Chinese Prosody.*

came into use, until finally, in the T'ang dynasty, one hundred and six rhymes were used, involving variations of both vowels and tones. These rhymes were collected into dictionaries, and, though the pronunciation of Chinese words has changed with the passing of the centuries, these classic rhymes are still used. Some of the rhymes persist unchanged.

In the fifth century Shên Yo (441–513 A.D.) first classified the Chinese tones for metrical purposes. The tones were divided into groups, called the *p'ing* and the *tsê* groups. The *p'ing* is a level, even tone, the *tsê* a variable tone.

With this work of Shên Yo, a second style of Chinese versification called *lü shih,* or "modern style," came into being, and quickly took its place beside the *ku shih* or "ancient style." In the *lü shih* the variations in arrangement and position of the *p'ing* and the *tsê* tones in the verse and the quatrain form the rhythm-scheme. Rhyme is also controlled in a measure by the tone system; for example, lines which do not rhyme must end on the tone opposite to that of the rhyme, and so on. *P'ing* rhymes are preferred.*

The *ku shih* may be divided into four classes, according to the length of its lines:

(1) Verses of four syllables. With a few exceptions, the *Book of Odes* is written in this style.

(2) Verses of five syllables. In the Han dynasty (about 140 B.C.) the five-syllable line came into use. It has been a favorite Chinese verse-form ever since.

---

* For detailed explanations, and for examples of the tone schemes, which vary greatly, see the works of Waley, Budd, Tsonming, De Harlez, and D'Hervey Saint-Denys.

(3) Verses of seven syllables. This verse may occur in alternation with shorter verses.

(4) Verses of a variable number of syllables—two, three, six, eight, and so on.

Poems in the *ku shih* may vary in length. The shortest consists of two verses. One *ku shih* poem, consisting of three hundred and ninety-five verses, is the longest piece of poetry in Chinese; composed by an unknown author under the Han dynasty, it is the tale of a beautiful maiden, who, though happily married, was so persecuted and harried by her mother-in-law and her parents that finally, in desperation, she drowned herself.

The *lü shih,* or "modern style" poetry, consists of verses of five or seven syllables each. Their rhythm is fixed by the tonal system outlined above.

In the *lü shih* the cæsura, or pause, comes after the second syllable in the five-syllable verse, and after the fourth syllable in the seven-syllable verse. This cæsura, however slight, is important in the grammatical interpretation of the verse. The poem may consist of four, six, or more such verses.

Since the introduction of the *lü shih,* both the *lü shih* and the *ku shih* have been indiscriminately used by the Chinese in their poetry, down to the present time. There are various other forms of Chinese poetry, the most important being the *tzu* and the *fu.* The former is a kind of song, in lines of varying length, and with a very elaborate tonal scheme. The *fu,* a composition in irregular meter, comes near our own "free verse." No translation of either of these forms appears in the present book.

THE PROBLEMS OF TRANSLATION

FEW OF THE MANY PROBLEMS involved in translating Chinese poetry into English verse confront the translator of poems from other languages. The question of form presents itself at the outset. The strict metrical system of the Chinese leads the translator at first to employ a strict metrical form in English. A certain degree of success may here and there be attained, but not sustained. A strain is put upon the fidelity of translation, words or phrases must be suppressed or added, and the translator finds that, if he desires to pursue this method long, he must borrow the bed of Procrustes. Some poems lend themselves readily to a smooth rhymed English, but more often a worthy rhyming version is impossible. Moreover, to obtain rhyme and regular length of line, one often sacrifices simplicity and clearness, vigor and directness.

Some well-known translators cling to the strict metrical form. Some go to the other extreme, and are satisfied with so-called "free verse." This usually contains none of the subtleties or beauties of the original, and it may easily be distorted out of all semblance to the original text. Still another group seeks to make a word-for-word, or, rather, a word-for-syllable translation. In view of the facility and frequency with which the Chinese poet transfers syllables and phrases from one verse to another, or from one part of a verse to another, for the sake of rhyme or rhythm, this treatment is inadequate, and often leads to grotesque English. Moreover, a single Chinese syllable may have many meanings in English. Unless the text is carefully restored to its original form before translation is begun, the meaning and intent of the author may remain obscure, or be entirely misinterpreted.

After many trials in these forms, the present translator has pursued the following method. The poem is carefully studied in the original. The text is restored to its original form as far as possible. A rough literal translation is then made, the meanings of each word and phrase being noted. After a few readings of this translation, the words and phrases fall into a pattern which, to the translator, appears to convey the proper meaning of the poem. The words and their meanings thus approximate the Chinese syllables and their connotations, as far as the differences in the two languages permit. This final translation should be in metrical English. The pattern may vary; invariable, however, is fidelity to the original text.

Strange as it may appear to one who has not studied Chinese, a poem is often susceptible of several translations, and each translation may be a faithful, scholarly presentation of the text. A comparison of various translations of any Chinese poem will reveal this. The only criteria in passing judgment should be the translator's knowledge of the language, and his acquaintance with Chinese history, character, environment, and life-experience. If he essays to cast his translation into metrical form, then the results are subject to criticism as English verse. This phase is not within the scope of the present study; only the Chinese original is considered.

Form is but one of the problems confronting the translator. In turning any piece of Continental literature into English, one finds the necessary literary aids at hand. With Chinese, all is different. Since the great *Chinese Dictionary* of Morrison, finished in 1822, many have been published, the most noteworthy in English being that of Giles; but none is complete in the number of words, definitions, or quoted examples of usage. It is necessary to turn to dictionaries in many other languages as well as to those in English, for no one is sufficient by itself. A translator who does not avail himself of the brilliant work of a Couvreur, a Karlgren, or a Schlegel—to mention but three—is precluded from interpreting Chinese poetry adequately.

The translator must divorce himself from the Western response to experience. He must approach his work subjectively, as a Chinese, seeing life through Chinese eyes, with the background of Chinese history, tradition, and culture. He dare not permit his Western interpretation of love or friendship or Nature to affect his translation. The Chinese attitude toward all these experiences must be his; otherwise he will fail, his work will be a distorted presentation of the original. The translation must be a faithful rendition of the poet's own words, so far as they can be brought over into English. Nothing must be read into them, and nothing left out. When translations cannot meet this test, they are not translations.

Similarly, the translator must limit himself to Chinese figures of speech. He is precluded from using Western simile and metaphor. He is deprived of the treasures of the vast storehouses of Western allusion, and must employ only the thesaurus of Chinese rhetoric. His translation will therefore be rich and adequate as his background is rich and his knowledge of Chinese rhetorical devices and allusions profound.

[31]

Finally, the most fascinating and interesting problem of translation is the interpretation of the ideograph.* Every Chinese syllable presents two problems. The first, comparatively simple, is the translation of the syllable by that English word or phrase which most nearly approximates it; the second is the study of the suggested potentialities of the ideograph. The poet often drives home his thought, and at the same time expresses an implication or a variation of emotional response, within the strokes of a single character. This may require several English words, a phrase, or even an entire sentence for its adequate elucidation. It must be constantly kept in mind that Chinese writing is, in the first analysis, a series of pictures of ideas. Inflections, tenses, articles, auxiliaries—most of these are lacking in the language, and must be supplied.

When the ideograph is examined, apart from the simple dictionary definition, implications of further meaning appear. These are the connotations of the ideograph, which induced the poet to use it in preference to another, as an English poet may use *dusk, twilight, sunset,* or *evening,* according to the shade of meaning which he desires to convey. In order to obtain a full and adequate translation of the ideograph, these implications must be considered. For example, there are several ideographs, each of which may be translated *morning, dawn,* or *sunrise.* One of them pictures the sun just above the horizon, another the newly-risen sun above the head of a man in armor, and still another the sun in a mist seen from a boat. In spite of the contention of some critics that the Chinese do

* A delightful book has been written by Karlgren on this subject—*Sound and Symbol in Chinese,* and Purcell has discussed it at length in his *Spirit of Chinese Poetry.*

[32]

not read their poems "etymologically," one is forced to consider, in translation, the choice of ideographs. Otherwise it is as though the French should translate our *dusk, twilight, sunset,* and *evening,* all by the one word *soir.* Of course, this principle of analyzing the ideograph can be pushed too far, until it becomes impractical and illusory, but to follow it is to come close to the genius of the Chinese language and the native interpretations of poetry throughout the centuries.

To the Occidental, handwriting is a means to an end—the expressing of a thought in an enduring form on paper. To the Chinese, calligraphy has been placed on an equality with painting, and an expert with the brush and ink-stone is honored equally with the artist. His ideographs are paintings—pictures, if you will—and when reading them he takes pleasure in their beauty of outline and in the pictures they bring to his eye, as much as in the simple "word-ideas" (if the term may be used) which they convey. We have to look rather far to see the *beech* in our modern *book,* but, as the ideograph for *night* is the picture of a roof with a man and the moon under it, we are not stretching our imagination, or risking the accusation of pedantry, in contending that the Chinese reader receives from this ideograph a richness of connotation greater than that of the word-idea *night.** This example is sufficient to show that the translator must give grave consideration to the composition of the syllables in his attempt to convey to the foreign reader the full meaning and intent of the poet.

* As Purcell says: "The Chinese written character, indeed, is so beautiful in itself, and its units so wrought about with subtleties, that a poem is but an elegant stringing together of minor poems, each one character long."—*The Spirit of Chinese Poetry.*

These, then, are the problems of the translator in a field which has been far from overcrowded. Thousands of beautiful lyrics still await translation, and every one that is given to us brings us closer to a real comprehension of the Chinese mind and spirit. More than this, each translation brings to our own culture an added richness, warmth, color, and depth.

ILLUSTRATIVE TRANSLATIONS

Artis poeticae est non omnia dicere.

Servius, *In Virgilii Aeneidos I*, 683.

"THE HUNDRED NAMES"

From break of day
Till sunset glow
I toil.
I dig my well,
I plow my field,
And earn my food
And drink.
What care I
Who rules the land
If I
Am left in peace?

THE PHILANDERER

When I gather the herbs in the land of Mei,
Do you know on whom my thoughts dwell?
On beautiful Mêng,
Of the house of Ch'i,
Who promised in Sang Chung
To meet me in Shang Kung,
And to go with me to Ch'i Shang.

When I gather the wheat in the north of Mei,
Do you know on whom my thoughts dwell?
On beautiful Mêng,
Of the house of I,
Who promised in Sang Chung
To meet me in Shang Kung,
And to go with me to Ch'i Shang.

When I gather the seed in the east of Mei,
Do you know on whom my thoughts dwell?
On beautiful Mêng,
Of the house of Yung,
Who promised in Sang Chung
To meet me in Shang Kung,
And to go with me to Ch'i Shang.

Book of Odes: I.4.4.

THE WIFE

My husband is far, far away
At the wars.
I know not when he'll come back to me,
Nor where he may be this day.

'Tis sunset.
The fowls roost in the holes in the wall,
The sheep and cattle come in from the field;
But my husband is far, far away
At the wars.
Can my thoughts be of anything
Save of him?

My husband is far, far away
At the wars.
The days and months seem
Without end.
The fowls nestle sleepily on their high roosts,
The cattle and sheep are safe in their barns;
But my husband is far, far away
At the wars.
Heaven keep from him
Hunger and thirst!

Book of Odes: I.6.3.

[39]

TO A HUSBAND

Since you and I
Exchanged the vows that made us one,
No shadow of distrust has marred our love.
Yet that hateful night
Crept on us unaware,
Put an end to happiness,
And tore you from my arms.

You, ever fearing, ever watching
For the hour of the march,
Stood long
Looking out into the night.
The bright stars had long since hidden
In the deep heavens,
And the heavy darkness hung blacker still.

You took me in your arms and said:
"Farewell!
The battle calls,
And only Heaven knows
If we shall ever meet again!"

How tight you held my hand!
I can see yet
The tear that fell upon it,
And those words you whispered last
I treasure still:

"Do not forget the hours of life and love
   That we have shared.
If I live,
I shall surely come back to you.
If I die,
Remember
That all my thoughts have always been of you."

TO ONE WHO HAS PASSED

Alas!
In vain I listen
For the rustle of your silks,
O my lady!

The dust lies thick
In the palace courts.
The fallen leaves are heaped
Against your locked and bolted door,
And your empty room
Is silent, cold, and still.

My poor heart can find no rest,
My lovely lady;
For you have gone forever,
And my longing is in vain.

DEATH OF LOVE

But yesterday
I loved,
And life was sweet.
I loved,
And my spirit soared
To heights undreamed.

To-day
The sun in vain
Shines on a darkened life,
A spirit pale and dead—
For love is done!

OTHER DAYS

As a gem set in gold,
As sweet music in tune,
As a sky strewn with stars
Was our life in our love.

As autumn leaves that, dying, fall,
As brooding clouds before the storm,
As a world bereft of stars and sun
Is my poor life since love has flown.

THE GARMENT OF MORTALITY

To-day
I sit in the halls of state.
To-morrow?
To-morrow I shall sleep
In the silence of the grave;
For my span of life
Now nears its latter end.

But when, or how,
Or in what form
I shall return,
It is not granted unto mortal man
To know.

CONSTANCY

My love for you
Is as the Northern Star,
That, fixed and steadfast,
Through the ages burns.
It is as the sun
That glows with white-hot flame,
And lights a world
That otherwise were dead.

THE DRUMS OF NIGHT

The night is long;
I cannot sleep.
I toss and turn
And hear the drums
Beat out the watches.

My thoughts are all
Of our first meeting
And our last farewell.

So I lie awake, alone,
And eat the bitter herb
Of heartbreak and neglect.

"THE FRAGRANT BLOSSOMS"

The air is clear;
The whole world
Glistens
In the moonlight.
We walk in the night, together,
You and I.

You sing,
And your song thrills me,
Plays upon my heartstrings,
And I sing "The Fragrant Blossoms"
In reply.

THE FROST

Young man,
Seize every minute
Of your time.
The days fly by;
Ere long you too
Will grow old.

If you believe me not,
See there, in the courtyard,
How the frost
Glitters white and cold and cruel
On the grass
That once was green.

REGRETS

The plum blossoms
Have fallen from the trees
And vanished quite;
The wind has flung the flowers
Of the willow
Far and wide.

The springtime of my years
Has vanished too,
And no friend remains
To answer to my call.

A SONG OF CHERRY-TIME

My heart is stirred to its depths
By the fan that you have sent
To remind me of our love.

Come to my chamber when you will,
My lord!
I await you with a longing
As ardent as your own.

A SONG

Is it only to-day
That we said farewell?
The lamp shines bright—
But it lights up
An empty room.

Ah! when will you come back
To me, my love?
My heart aches
For the lonely days
To come.

SONG OF SONGS

I feast my eyes upon you
As you lie
With arms outstretched
Upon your couch.
Your hair, undone,
Flows down in shining waves
Upon your snow-white breast.

O my love!
There is no part of you
That does not stir
The swift and flaming passion
Of my love.

THROUGH YOUR WINDOW

I watched your red lips move
In song,
And your jade-like fingers pluck
The stringèd lute.

Love urged me on—
To enter,
Take you in my arms,
Make you my own.

But I blushed, I trembled,
I dared not move—
And now
It is too late!

TO HIM I LOVE

Do you not see
That you and I
Are as the branches
Of one tree?
With your rejoicing
Comes my laughter;
With your sadness
Start my tears.
Love,
Could life be otherwise
With you and me?

WEAVING

As I sit at the loom
And weave,
I dream of you,
My lord!
.

I recall the day
When first we met,
And how, from that glad hour,
Our two hearts
Have beat as one.

Strange—
That, try as I will,
The threads all break,
And I can't throw my shuttle
Straight.

LONELINESS

Since the day
You left me here alone,
My love,
The world's grown old and gray,
The clear green jade
Has lost its sheen,
And the gold is dim and dull;

For you are to me
The sun and moon,
Which come forth in turn
To light my nights and days.

DEVOTION

Since you are gone,
And I am here alone,
My chest of rich brocades
Stands long untouched.
My love for you
Is as the ceaseless winds
That blow across the world
Both night and day.

A DREAM

I dreamed last night
The gates of Heaven opened wide,
And you came forth.

You stood beside my bed,
More wondrous fair
Than ever were
The nymphs of far Wu Shan.
Your eyes were sad.
Your soul
Seemed to enfold and possess mine.
Your lips moved,
And your loved voice spoke, and said:
"In the night
Your long sighs called me,
And I came."
You ceased, and, bowing low,
You smoothed my pillow,
Brought me food and drink,
And bade me rest.

I closed my eyes,
And, when I looked again,
Your form had vanished
In the shadow and the gloom,
And only night was with me,
And the silence of the night.

I awoke,
And could not stay the tears
That mourn you,
And never shall cease mourning,
While I live.

TO ONE AFAR

It is spring,
And somewhere in the night
A lute is playing.
It sings of youth and joy and love.

But what can it mean to me
When my heart is with you,
A thousand li away?

CALM OF EVENING

Though the sun has set
Behind the city walls,
Its afterglow
Still lingers
In my room.
The peace of twilight
Whispers
In the pines,
And
The throbbing of a lute
Comes from afar.

SINCE YOU ARE GONE

Since you are gone,
Even the fragrant yü
Has drooped and withered
In its jasper bowl.
No matter where I turn,
Your shadow seems to linger there,
And, when the night creeps on,
My restless sleep
Brings dreams of you
So far away.

SONG OF THE FOUR COLORS

Red as the sky
That at sunset glows
Beyond the city walls.

Green as the pine
That rises pure
Out of the swirling mists.

Black as the cloud
That threatens rain
On a gloomy autumn day.

White as the snow
That heaps in drifts
On fabled Yao Chi's shore.

JOY

In fair Lo Yang,
When you left my side,
The snow fell blossom-like
Far and wide.

Now that you have come,
The spring winds blow,
And the fragrant blossoms
Fall like snow.

THE SPRING WIND

Though I cannot see
The wind of spring,
I hear its murmur everywhere,
Now loud, now soft,
Now dying quite away.

It plays around my mirror,
Full of mischief,
And blows my rouge and powder
All about,
Then dances merrily away,
To hold low whispered converse
With my lute.

ON SEEING A BEAUTIFUL WOMAN
RIDE BY IN A CART

What gentle looks!
What a lovely slender waist
And shapely arm!
What witchcraft
In your smile and voice,
That lift me
To the clouds!

Unknown, unknowing,
You ride down the street,
And never see me
Gaze into your face.
If now I worship you,
Not knowing who you are,
What would I do
If my wish should be granted
And you should be my love?

A MARCHING SONG

To find a thousand cattle
For the taking
In the fields,
To lie
Beside a shady spring
With a hundred jars of wine,
To go hunting on the mountains
Every morning
As we please,
To be welcomed every evening
By another light-o'-love;
What ho, for the life of a soldier!

FORSAKEN

I tear the jade pins
From my hair,
And fling my jeweled flowers
On the floor.
In the bright moonlight,
Fanned by the cool spring wind,
I weep alone,
And wish that I might die!

MELANCHOLY

The night itself seems sad,
And neither peace nor sleep will come.
Restless, I rise and look out
On the terrace facing south.
The moon shines down upon the roofs
With clear cold gleam,
And the fallen leaves
Stir with strange whisperings in the wind.
I play upon my shêng.
Only a few chill notes
Come from its circled pipes.
I pluck my lute,
But the taut dry strings
Protest in dull and melancholy chords.
I sit and dream of what has been,
And of the myriad woes
That man is called upon to bear
In one short life.

Ah, where can I find a mirror
Bright enough
To show me the true image
Of my sad and aching heart?

THE TRYST

I wait in the night
Where shadows creep
Before the rising moon,
And the wind is sweet
With the fragrance of fields afar.

Oh, when will you come, my heart?
The hours are long.
Hope wipes the tears
From my anxious eyes;
Then doubt brings them back again.

THE CALL OF SPRING

The morning glow creeps over
The forests of the north.
The first flowers of the year
Make of the grass
A brilliant green brocade.

When spring is here,
And all is fair,
Why must I sit alone,
Indoors,
And unceasing ply
The shuttle of my loom?

FAITH

Ever since the day
You left me here alone,
The flame in the golden incense-bowl
Is dead;
But my love for you
Is like a torch
Burning clearly
Through the watches of the night.

A SONG OF
MO SHANG SANG

Silent and tearful,
I watch you go
Down the mountain path.
Your road will take you far from me,
To the Empire's distant wall.

As for me,
A mere woman—
I turn sadly back,
To sit and wait
In an empty room!

CONFESSION

To-day, in the hall,
I came upon her—mere concubine!—
Who replaced me in my husband's heart.

I fled out of doors,
And met him face to face.

I tried to look composed,
Threw back my sleeve,
Waved my moon-round fan—
And failed.
I hesitated,
Tried to speak,
But the unwilling words
Stuck in my throat, refused to come.
Try as I would to hold back
The pearl-like tears,
They welled from my downcast lids,
And then I knew
That I loved him still,
And that the pain
Which grips my heart to-day
Would never, never cease.

THE SENTRY

First
watch

The soldiers beat the hour
On their empty copper pots,
And sentry calls to sentry
Along the city walls.
From the distance comes the clank of arms,
The stamp of hoofs,
Men tramping in the dark,
And all the roar and clatter
Of an army on the march.

Second
watch

The drum beats out the second watch.
The long, chill night
Enwraps the city streets.
I grip my bow the tighter—
Good bow, curved as the crescent moon—
And grasp my sword
That to my touch
Is chill and damp as frost.

Third
watch

The third dreary watch has sounded,
When all the night
Seems full of hidden, fearsome things.
To cheer myself I hum a tune,
A song of sunny spring,

"The Blossoms of the Plum Tree Fall to Earth."
I doze an instant,
And my heart straightway
Is with a maid
In a willow grove, at home.

*Fourth
watch*

The fourth watch has crept slowly on.
The moon has sunk behind great banks of cloud,
The stars hang low in the Milky Way,
And on the cold north wind
Comes the faint, far-off blast of a Tartar horn,
And the neighing of a horse.

*Fifth
watch*

At last!
The trumpet sounds the morning call!
The first crimson light of dawn
Now glows on the topmost mountain peak,
And the birds begin to chirp
High up on the city wall.
The long, long night is ended,
And we go to rest,
Weary and silent,
Down the steep stone tower steps.

THE SLAVE

Who is that sad-eyed slave
In the harlot's house?

All the long day
She sits at the open window,
And plays on a jade-green lute.
Her face is fair
As the sun at dawn,
And her robes are of rainbow hue.

At the sound of her voice
The great wild goose
Stops short in his headlong flight,
And the cuckoo ceases his carefree call,
To mourn her tragic fate.

But, alas!
Her song is carried away
On the wings of the swift east wind,
And no one hears
And no one heeds
The cry of her breaking heart.

A DIRGE

We enter our earthly bodies
But to suffer,
And all mortals
Live a life of pain and woe.
Our heart and spirit
Bow in grief and anguish;
Our food
Is often the herb of bitterness.
Fortune
Brings cares and worries,
And our portion
Is oftener fear than joy.
For a brief time only
Do we see the glow of morning,
And the lamp that burns at evening
Fades and dies.
All is over.
We are gathered back to earth,
And the struggle for long years,
Fame, or fortune,
Is in vain.

A BOWL OF WINE

One by one
The petals fall
Into the green jade bowl.
Lightly they float,
And their kisses
Perfume the fragrant wine.

TO HSÜ LING

If you think well of me,
And ever would be kind,
Be so to-day
While I yet live upon this earth.

Do not wait to hear the sobbing flutes
Behind my bier,
On my last journey
Down the sunlit mountain road.

LONGING

You are a flower
In far Lo Yang,
I a willow in
Wu Ch'ang—
And the spring winds
Are laden
With our sighs.

When, ah! when,
Shall we walk again,
Hand held in hand,
You and I?

FACING DEATH

Unreal!
Unreal are both creation
And destruction,
And man's body
Is illusion and a dream.

It is the house
Where for a space
Sojourn his heart and mind;
But seek not there
For man's real self—
It does not dwell therein.

WELCOME HOME!

How swift was your departure,
How slow your coming home!
Let's drink deeply of the good warm wine,
And drown the years between!

THE RETURN OF SPRING

Though I'm sad unto death,
The tears refuse to come,
And my long-drawn sighs
Are changed to joyous song.

The flowers in the courtyard
Spread their colors to the sun:
Can I forever grieve and sorrow
When spring calls loud and long?

A LETTER

Pearls!
Twin pearls,
Bright gems of ocean,
To me, a married woman,
You have sent!

Yet you know I have a husband
In attendance, in the palace,
On the Lord of Light, the Emperor—
May he live ten thousand years!

But the thought that prompted you
I cherish
In my bosom with the jewels.
There they've lain hidden till this hour,
In the soft, enfolding silk.

I know—you need not tell me—
That your thoughts are pure as moonlight,
Or as the glowing sun at midday
Overhead.

My home lies noble in its gardens.
There the marriage oath I've taken,
And I ever shall be faithful,
Even past the gates of death.

So!—
The twin pearls are in this letter.
I send them back to you in sadness
With a sigh.

If you look closely, you'll find with them
Two other twin gems lying,
Twin tears fallen from my eyelids,
Telling of a breaking heart.

Alas, that perverse life so willed it
That we met too late, after
I had crossed my husband's threshold
On that fateful wedding day!

ABSENCE

Ever since the day
You went,
And left me here alone,
My lord,
The world is changed!

Upon the loom
The web, half woven, hangs
Untouched.

My thoughts
Are all of you,
And I am like yon silver moon,
Whose glory wanes
And grows more pale
Each night!

DAYDREAMS

Far away on the old city walls
The willows
Are clouds of gray.
Row on row
The mulberries grow,
All clad in robes of green.

Yesternight I dreamed—
How sweet that dream!—
Of you in far Yü Yang.
And all the while
My gathered leaves
Lie wilting in the sun!

THE YEARS BETWEEN

So,
After all these long, long years,
You have come back!

How changed!
Your jade-like face
Now lined with grief,
Your hair to silver turned!

But who can see
On my sad heart
The scars graved deep,
The unhealed wounds
Of the bitter years between?

FAREWELL

The setting sun
Shines on the village
At the river's mouth,
And the spring wind
Softly stirs
The snow-white blossoms
On the bank.

We've said
Our last farewells,
And now
You're floating
Down the stream.

Why does the twilight
Come so fast?—
Or is it the mist?
For I scarce can see
Your figure
In the fast-receding
Boat.

THE HOUSE OF CHUNG

In the north city
Stands the house of Chung,
A wealthy man.

Not long ago, his wife lay dead.
Guests and mourners
Thronged the spacious halls,
Condoled with him,
And sat at his board,
Laden with food and drink.

To-day, old Chung himself lies dead,
And of all those many guests
Who ate his meat and drank his wine,
Not one comes to shed a tear!
How cold is the heart of man!

NIGHTFALL

The night comes on;
The river road grows dark.
The peasants come in slowly
From the fields.
In a hut hid deep
Amid the towering trees
Glows a tiny flame
To guide a husband home.

HOME FROM THE WARS

My lord will soon be here!
I stand
Beneath the age-old trees
Of Chu Lang's shrine
And wait—how long the waiting!—
And watch the sunlight
Slowly fade,
The shadows grow
And darken into night.

Hark!
From the river bank
Come sounds of flutes,
And merry songs of welcome.
He has come!

CUPS OF JADE

Where the lotus pool
Is fragrant with its flowers,
We drank our last farewell
From cups of jade.

You thought I shunned you
When I, quickly turning,
Hid my face from you,
And would not look again.

Ah!
Being but a man,
How could you know, belovèd,
That it was to wipe
The scalding tears away?

GIFTS

I gave you
A fine new green silk gown;
You gave me
A clasp of jade.

I thought
To adorn your slender form;
But you
Clasped my heart, cruel maid!

TEARS

The hours drag.
Sleepless,
I turn and toss
The livelong night,
And long for you.

If you do not believe me,
Look!
You'll find
My pillow wet
With the traces of my tears.

YEARNING

A golden bowl
In which to wash these hands?
To burn incense,
To intone prayers
At mighty Buddha's shrine?
What vain things are these
That life has brought
To me,
When all I crave is,
To be held close
In your arms!

ALONE

The vast world
Is still and silent
All about me.
The east wind is stirring
In the blossoms
By the border of the pool,
And the earth
Is crimson
With their fallen petals.

I sit and dream
Of you, my love,
So far away,
And, unawares,
A pearl—a teardrop—
Falls
Upon my hand.

THE MIRROR

The years depart,
And steal away
The rosy cheeks
Of youth.
Sorrows come,
And bring with them
White hair.

At dawn to-day
I opened wide
My mirror case,
And looked.
Was it my own
Or another's face
That met
My startled gaze?

LAMENT FOR A DEAD
WINE-MAKER

Poor old Chi has died and gone
To the distant Yellow Springs;
I'll wager
He still makes his good wine there!

But the warm sun never shines
In that faraway land,
So who'll call
For his spring wine rare?

THE YELLOW CRANE TOWER

It is evening
In the month of May;
Weary and footsore,
I reach Chang Sha,
The city by the stream.

In the Tower of the Yellow Crane
I hear a jade flute piping
"The Falling Blossoms of the Plum,"
And I look toward home,
Afar in the gloom,
To the westward of Chang An.

YOUTH RIDES FORTH

Into Chin Shih
East of Wu Ling
Came a band of young men,
Prancing.
The horses they bestrode
Were snow-white,
And silver-mounted
Were their saddles.
Ever as they rode,
The cool spring wind
Rained blossoms
All about them.

Who knows whither, or how far
They ride?

Laughing, the maid
Waves to them;
Then, turning,
Enters the tavern,
To set out the wine again.

A DRINKING BOUT

How long have I been lying asleep,
Here on the fragrant grass?
The sun is already setting
Behind me in the west.
There lie my jug and wine-cup
Overturned upon the ground,
And my guest!—
He must have departed long ago!

I cannot remember picking flowers,
Yet my hands are both quite full!
How did they ever come?

PEONIES

How I should love
To lie among the peonies
And drink to my heart's content!
But, alas!
If the flowers could speak,
I fear they would say:
"We do not blossom for old men."

AUTUMN LEAVES

The years that pass
Have brought with them
White hair.
Autumn has come,
And the trees stand
Bare and cold.

Perplexed,
I ask the yellow leaves:
"Are you, too, sad?
What griefs have you,
That you
Are sere and old?"

SLEEPLESS

Outside the palace windows
The fireflies flit in the shadows.
Within the halls
All sounds of life have ceased,
And, in the silken courts
Where the women dwell,
The autumn night stands guard.
Of all the lamps within these walls,
Mine alone keeps vigil
Till the dawn.

TO CHU TA

So you're leaving now,
To travel to Wu Ling!
I bring you this gift,
A precious sword,
To speed you on your way.

But, though worth its weight
In purest gold,
Such a gift
Means naught to you and me,
Whose lives
Are but the sharing of our hearts.

PUPPETS

The marionettes
Are carved of wood.
Endowed with life
When the strings are pulled,
They look,
With their wrinkled skin
And thin white hair,
Like real old men;

But, when the play is over
And the scene is changed,
They lie lifeless,
Without movement, without breath.

So man is born,
And passes like a puppet
Through the dream-play
We call life.

MOONLIGHT ON THE
WEST TOWER

It is the third watch
Of the night.
The wind stirs softly
In the lotuses,
And the dewdrops
On their petals
Gleam like pearls.

As I sit
And dream
Of our short happiness,
And of the cruel fate
That tore you
From my arms,
My eyes are filled with tears,
And the silent lute
Slips
From my unheeding hands.

A GLIMPSE INTO A
COURTYARD

A green bird,
With a grape in its beak,
Lights
On the metal well-curb.

A pretty maiden,
Startled,
Runs indoors,
And does not even dare
To lift her curtain
And look out!

A LAMENT FOR MY SON TS'UI

You were a pearl
In the palm of my hand,
My tiny baby boy.

Why is it that I,
A white-haired man of three-score years,
Am left behind,
And you, a child of three,
Must by Heaven's silent, stern decree,
Precede me
To that strange and far-off land
Of death?

My heart is wounded sore,
But not with a blade of steel;
My old eyes are dimmed and dull,
But not with the dust of earth.

These arms
That held you closely to my breast
Are empty now,
And I mourn, as did Têng Yu of old,
My only son.

A FORSAKEN GARDEN

I enter the court
Through the middle gate—
And my sleeve is wet with tears.

The flowers still grow
In the courtyard,
Though two springs have fled
Since last their master came.

The windows, porch, and bamboo screen
Are just as they always were,
But at the entrance to the house
Someone is missing—
You!

PLANTING A LICHI TREE

The red fruit of the lichi
Is as precious as the pearl.

Here I stand,
An agèd, white-haired man,
And plant a lichi
In my courtyard!

How can I know
Who will be here
When ten more years
Have come and gone?

What a fool I am!

NIGHT ON THE WEST RIVER

No moon
To light my way upon the stair,
Cold comfort
In the wine I drink alone.

Black clouds,
Rain,
The hurried flight of birds,
Water flowing grayly
In the dusk.

A rising storm,
Boats tugging at their mooring ropes.
Sails full-spread
To take advantage of the wind.

A moving point of fire
In the dark,
The distant lantern
Of a passing boat.

THE ALMOND BLOSSOMS OF
CHAO VILLAGE

For fifteen long years,
Times without number
I have come
To see the red almond-blossoms
Open in the spring.

Now I am growing old—
I am all of seventy-three,
And it is hard for my old legs
To come thus far.

I fear that this time
Is the last,
And I have come
To bid the red blossoms of the almond
A long farewell.

DRUNK AGAIN

Last year, when I lay sick,
I vowed
I'd never touch a drop again
As long as I should live.

But who could know
Last year
What this year's spring would bring?

And here I am,
Coming home from old Liu's house
As drunk as I can be!

ON BEING STRICKEN WITH PARALYSIS

Good friends,
Why waste your time in wailing
And in sympathy for me?

Surely, from time to time,
I shall be strong enough
To move about a bit.
As for travel,
On land there are carrying-chairs,
And on the water there are boats;
So, if I can but keep my courage,
What need have I of feet?

HOMESICK

The waters of Wei
Flow to the east,
Toward home!
Two tears
From my eyes
Fall into the stream,
And are borne away.

O tears,
Greet my garden,
So dear to me,
When at last
You reach Yung Chou!

SPRING DREAMS

Last night, as I slept,
The spring wind tiptoed
Into my room,
Bringing dreams.
And my dream
Was of her I love,
Far, far away,
South of the waters of Hsiang.
And, as I tossed on my pillow,
In that instant,
Borne on the wings of the wind,
I was transported a thousand li,
Even to the land of Hsiang.

WAITING

I stand and watch
The moonlight creep
Through the great gate
Across the court.
I cannot sleep!

A stir in the night!
Is it you, my lord,
Come to my arms at last?

Ah!
'Tis but the shadow
Of dancing flowers,
High on the garden wall.—
And still I watch
And wait!

WISE AGE TO YOUTH

Wear your gold and silken garments;
Store not one of them away;
Flaunt them in your years of beauty
Ere the world grows old and gray.

Pluck the blossoms in the springtime
When they open to the sun,
For you'll find but withered branches
When bright youth and love are done.

THE CHARIOTS GO FORTH
TO WAR

The chariots go forth to war,
Rumbling, roaring as they go;
The horses neigh and whinny loud,
Tugging at the bit.
The dust swirls up in great dense clouds,
And hides the Han Yang bridge.

In serried ranks the archers march,
A bow and quiver at each waist;
Fathers, mothers, children, wives
All crowd around to say farewell.
Pulling at clothes and stamping feet,
They force the soldiers' ranks apart,
And all the while their sobs and cries
Reach to the skies above.

"Where go you to-day?" a passer-by
Calls to the marching men.
A grizzled old veteran answers him,
Halting his swinging stride:

"At fifteen I was sent to the north
  To guard the river against the Hun;
At forty I was sent to camp,
  To farm in the west, far, far from home.
When I left, my hair was long and black;
  When I came home, it was white and thin.
To-day they send me again to the wars,
  Back to the north frontier,
By whose gray towers our blood has flowed
  In a red tide, like the sea—
And will flow again, for Wu Huang Ti
  Is resolved to rule the world.

"Have you not heard how in far Shantung
  Two hundred districts lie
With a thousand towns and ten thousand homes
  Deserted, neglected, weed-grown?
Husbands fighting or dead, wives drag the plow,
  And the grain grows wild in the fields.
The soldiers recruited in Shansi towns
  Still fight; but, with spirit gone,
Like chickens and dogs they are driven about,
  And have not the heart to complain.

"I am greatly honored by your speech with me.
   Dare I speak of my hatreds and grief?

"All this long winter, conscription goes on
   Through the whole country, from the east to the west,
   And taxes grow heavy. But how can we pay,
   Who have nothing to give from our land?
   A son is a curse at a time like this,
   And daughters more welcome far;
   For, when daughters grow up, they can marry, at least,
   And live on a neighbor's land.
   But our sons? We bury them after the fight,
   And they rot where the grass grows long.

"Have you not seen at far Ching Hai,
   By the waters of Kokonor,
   How the heaped skulls and bones of slaughtered men
   Lie bleaching in the sun?
   Their ancient ghosts hear our own ghosts weep,
   And cry and lament in turn;
   The heavens grow dark with great storm-clouds,
   And the specters wail in the rain."

THE FIREFLIES

At Wu Shan, of an autumn night,
The fireflies come flitting
Through the curtains
Into my room,
And flutter on my garments.
So warm they seem
That my lute and book
Are chill to my touch
In the dark.
They settle on the walls and eaves,
And my room is agleam as with stars.
They circle round the courtyard,
And, in clusters,
Cling to the old stone well-curb.
They enter the flowers
And make of each a tiny, glowing jewel.
I stand, an old, white-haired man,
By the broad Yang Tze,
And watch you, little fireflies,
And wonder if, when next year comes,
I shall be here to greet you.

THE PARROT

The parrot sits
Upon his perch,
Wrapped in gloomy thought,
And dreams
Of his distant home.
His wings of brightest blue
Are clipped;
From his red beak
Come words of wisdom.
Will they never, never
Unlatch his cage,
And set him free once more?
Impatient, in anger,
He claws and tears at his perch,
To which he has clung
So long.
Will the world of men
Not pity him,
And the freedom he has lost?
Of what use to him in prison
Is his coat of wondrous hue?

WAR

Out of the northeast
A white horse galloped,
Aquiver with fear,
And pierced was his empty saddle
By two long, deadly arrows.

What of his rider now,
And where the vain courage
That spurred him to combat—
And to death?

At midnight
Went forth the order
To give battle to the foe;
But for him it was the command to die!

Ah, many a home this day
In vain
Mourns for its fallen son,
And a wailing that rises to Heaven
Goes forth,
And bitter tears flow
Like the icy rains
Of winter!

SUCCESS

I ask you, my friend,
What ought a man want
But to sit with his wine
In the sun?

My neighbors all come to talk over the news,
And to settle the problems of state.
I've no taxes to pay
On my house or my field.
I'm lucky, you say?
So I am!
My three sons?
Married, all of them;
Fine wives they've got,
And from the best families, too!

My daughters?
I've five of them, all wed.
Good husbands I found for them,
And every one rich!

So I sit in the sun
With my jug of old wine,
And I'd not change with the lords of the land!

A VISIT

Over our cups of wine,
In the arbor by the stream,
We talked and talked,
Until it seemed
As if we had left no subject
In all the world, from east to west,
Untouched.

And now my cart has rumbled off,
And when I turn my head
To see you once again,
You are lost to sight, old friend,
Hidden
By the autumn rain.

THE GRAND CANAL

The waters of the Grand Canal
Flow blue as the sky,
And the east wind sighs
In the willow trees.

You have just arrived;
We have hardly met—
And now
You must leave again!

Oh, the pain,
The fullness of the cup
Of bitterness
That parting brings!

NEWS FROM HOME?

You have come from my native village?
You surely have news for me!
Does the sun still peep in my window?
Are there buds on the old plum tree?

NO NEWS

My home is in Mêng Chin village,
Where the Huang Hô flows to the sea.
Boats often come to the southward;
Will they never bring letters to me?

NANKING

It is raining on the river
Everywhere.
The long grass at the water's edge
Bows low before
The flail of the cloud-swept sky.

The great line of kings
Has passed away.
No more are they
Than a ghostly dream,
Or the cry of a bird
In the night.

Gray and unrecking,
The city wall stands.
It is not moved
By the shadow-show,
Nor are the trees
That bow their heads
And stretch out their arms
To the rain
On the long, long river dyke.

RIDING TO TSAN SHIH

The dark shades of sunset
Creep over forest and court.
In the west corridors
The gauze lanterns
Are agleam.

Under a spreading pine
Sits a priest from the hills,
Alone,
Lost in deep meditation.

EVENTIDE

When I move,
My silken garments
Spread their fragrance,
Sweet as incense.

The red water-lilies
Wave like tassels
In the autumn twilight haze.

A fresh breeze
Stirs the fleecy clouds
That cling about the mountain tops,
And the willows by the pool
Bow low,
And gently kiss the water
With
Their slender, bright-green leaves.

THE WEST RIVER

It is spring,
And ten thousand maple trees
Are clad in new green leaves.
Under the old red bridge
A sailboat glides
Into the sunset glow.

My thoughts
Are afar with you,
My love,
Afar
Where the West River's waters,
Night and day,
Flow unceasing
To the sea.

A DESERTED TEMPLE

The wind sweeps down the mountain side,
Heaping the snow in great white drifts.

There stands a temple,
Long deserted and in ruins.
No smoke arises;
The courts are empty,
And the gates
Have long since fallen in decay.

But, in the night,
When all is calm,
The bright moonlight creeps
Through the silent courts
And looks down upon
The ancient fallen shrine.

GREEN SPRING

The spring day is clad in brightest green.
The morning sun
Floods the hills in golden glory.
From early morn till dusk
The garden is filled with nodding flowers
Of every shade and hue.
We walk to and fro,
And laugh and sing,
And discuss philosophy,
Or gaze afar
And drink our fill of nature's beauty.

Suddenly comes a knock at the garden gate.
Hasten!
The guest of honor has arrived!
With grave and old-fashioned ceremony
We greet him,
Raising high
The three ritual cups of wine.

RAIN

The turning of the year
Has come.
It is the tenth day,
And the rain falls ceaselessly.
It seems an age
Since last the sun appeared,
And still
There is no sign
Of clearing skies.

The old man cannot sleep.
Restless, he rises,
Looks out at the door,
And, with a sigh,
Lies down again
Upon his bed.
There, with the patience
Of old age,
He listens
To the monotone of rain,
Pattering through the leaves,
Upon the window frame.

A VISIT WITH YANG CHI

A heavy snow is falling.
The cold is cruel and bitter,
And the house is chill.
We sit up, reading,
Through the long watches of the night,
And drink old wine,
Warm with the fires of spring.

The first bottle greets Confucius,
And with him wise old Mencius;
The next summons their disciples,
Tz'u Kung and grave Yen Hui.
Another bottle follows,
And another,
And we enter the wondrous world of poets
And their dreams.

Through the night
We read together.
At break of dawn we climb the stairs,
And from the tower-top
Look out upon a world of snowy jade.

DESPAIR

Who dares play a flute so early
By my window,
When the world is scarce astir?

Alas!
It has called me from forgetful sleep
To the world of care again.

How my heart aches to hear the song,
An echo from that long-lost dream
Of life and love
With you!

Strange, that the piping lay
Of a shepherd lad
Should be for me
The funeral dirge of love!

SUNDOWN

The yellow sunset has faded
In the courtyard,
And the rain
Begins to fall.

I sit alone
By my tiny lamp,
And try to sew;
But, weary of my work,
And with hands idle
In my lap,
I lose myself in dreams.

Outside,
The chill wind seems to shear
The dead leaves
From the t'ung tree,
Like a knife.

OLD FRIENDS

The two old men
Sit in silence together,
Living in dim memories
Of the past.
They are lifelong friends
And need no words
To share their thoughts.

One quavers to the other:
"May you live a hundred years,
And may I live ninety-nine."

The other nods his old white head
And gravely says:
"Let us go home together
And drink a cup of wine."

WANDERING AT NIGHT

I wander at random, silent, alone,
Through the empty, ghostly city,
Where even the birds
Have long since gone to rest.

I look up from earth to heaven.
The clouds have melted away,
Save one long wisp,
Trailing across the deep, clear blue.

A chill creeps over the world,
Driving out the day's fierce heat,
And in the huai trees
The wind whispers and stirs,
And the dead blossoms fall
Like rain.

A HAPPY OLD MAN

The water murmurs
In the old stone well,
And, a rippling mirror,
Gives back the clear blue sky.
The river roars,
Swollen with the late rains of spring.
On the cool, jade-green grass
The golden sunshine
Splashes.

Sometimes, at early dawn,
I climb
Even as far as Lien Shan Temple.
In the spring
I plow the thirsty field,
That it may drink new life.
I eat a little,
I work a little.
Each day my hair grows thinner,
And, it seems,
I lean ever a bit more heavily
On my old thornwood cane.

EVENING AT THE INN OF
YÜN MÊNG

With book forgotten,
I sit dreaming,
And look out
Toward the west.

A wild goose
From the north
Flies overhead.
One by one
The t'ung-tree leaves
Flutter and fall
By the well,
And in the pond
The dead, dry lotus-stems
Rustle and stir in the wind.
The night comes on,
And with the night the rain,
Tapping, whispering gently
At the window and the door.

The year has reached its eventide,
And soon will pass away.

HALFWAY UP
THE MOUNTAIN

I look down
Upon the world,
Spread below me
In the setting sun.

Out of the shadowy forest
Winds the road
By which I came,
Deserted.

Even as I gaze,
A bank of cloud
Sweeps down,
And, at a stroke,
Blots out the world.

But, far above me,
In the sun's last rays,
Still gleams
The topmost peak.

AFLOAT ON THE LAKE

The first cool breeze of autumn
Scarcely ruffles
The mirror of the lake.
Bright and peaceful
Rises the moon
Where, dark on the shore,
Stands a lone tree.
From a distant hamlet
Gleams a single lamp.
A wild goose, overhead,
Flits by like a shadow.
A fish leaps from the water,
Showering bright drops
In the moonlight,
And with a slight sound
Falls back into the pool.

I lean on my oar,
And, drifting along,
Lose myself
In vague visions
And dreams.

THE BOOKWORM

The musty tomes
Are heaped high on your shelves.
You read them
Like the worm that bores them through.
Yet the greatest thoughts
And wisdom of mankind
Are found only in the book of human life.

MOONLIGHT ON THE
HAN RIVER

The clouds of sunset
Gather in the western sky,
And over the silent silvery Han
Rises a white jade moon.

Not often does life
Bring such beauty.

Where shall I see the moon
Next year?

CLIMBING TUNG KUAN
MOUNTAIN

The mountain path
Is steep and strait.
It is autumn,
And the yellow leaves
Flutter slowly to their rest.
The sunlight
Through the forest pines
Splashes gold upon the earth.
The birds seem numberless;
Their calls
Fill the forest aisles with joy,
And the gentle winds
Are sweet
With the scent
Of wild chrysanthemums.

THE POOL

The pool is radiant
With the lotus plants.
Their broad green leaves
Sway to and fro
In the cool wind of dusk.

It brings back to me
The clear image of a lake,
Where, long ago,
Alone in the twilight,
I poled my way
Among the flowers,
Fanned by soft, perfumed winds.

EVENING AT CHUNG SHAN

A misty rain is falling
In the village
By the stream.
In the cold wind
The lilac blossoms fall,
And the sand
Is hidden
In a snowdrift
Of crimson petals.

Dreaming in my bamboo hut
By the hibiscus hedge,
I look out upon
The dismal world.

No one stirs
In the gloom,
Only,
Now and then,
From the warmth of a wine shop
A muffled figure hurrying home.

THE PLUM TREE

Over a corner of the wall
The old plum tree stretches out its arms.
Though the world is still held in frosty thrall,
It has wakened
From its wintry sleep
And put forth pure white blossoms.

At first glance,
From a distance,
They looked like heaped-up, powdered snow,
Until the spring wind
Brought me
The message of their fragrance.

✳GREETINGS!

Under the blossoms,
With a jug of wine,
I watch the clouds sail by.
My thoughts are all of you,
Old friend,
As I raise my cup on high!

THE TEMPLE BELLS OF YÜN SUI

In the shadow of the tall bamboos
The tangled grass grows green,
And the old road, long deserted,
Is weed-grown.

To guide me on my weary way,
The kindly, thoughtful wind
Sends the chimes of far-off music
Through the rain.

RETURNING

The day is done.
Back to their folds
Come ox and sheep.

Just as the drum
Beats the sunset hour,
I reach the shore.
Swift on the stream
Creep the mist and the dark.
To my ear comes the thud
Of a passing oar.
A great fish leaps
In sudden fear.
Dimly seen,
A ghostly sail flits by.

The wind from the north
Sweeps down on the world.
The night is come.

HU CHIU SHAN

See! There stands the temple
Where I worship,
Its tower pointing skyward,
High story heaped on story,
The great shrine of Hu Chiu Shan.

Watching from my window
In the darkness,
When all is peace and silence,
I see the oil lamps burning
To the gods of Hu Chiu Shan.

When on the altar
Burns sweet incense,
I know great Buddha will bless me,
For gold and jewels I have given
To the priests of Hu Chiu Shan.

CAREFREE

What fun it is
On a summer or an autumn day,
When all the rains have fled away,
To go boating on the lake.

From my calabash jug
I drink good old wine
Until I am jolly drunk.

Then I lie on my back
Where the lotus buds nod,
And watch the gulls
Wheel through the blue.

BUTTERFLIES

The blossoms fall like snowflakes
On the cool, deep, dark-green moss,
They lie in white-heaped fragrant drifts
Before the courtyard gates.

The butterflies, not knowing
That the days of spring are done,
Still pursue the flying petals
Across the garden wall.

THE WINE SHOP

By Hsi Tzu Lake
Stands a wine shop,
Its flag waving bravely
In the breeze.

A man goes out
With a well filled jug,
Singing merrily
As he goes.

He climbs the road
Through the apricot trees,
All ablossom on the hill.
Though he's out of sight,
Round a turn in the road
I can hear him singing on.

TO MY MOTHER

Day after day
I have climbed the hill
To watch for your letter.
In vain!

To-day
The wild chrysanthemums
Blossomed yellow
On the hedge,
To comfort my sad heart
And bid me hope.

THE KEEPSAKE

I have a pin
Of purest yellow gold.
It adorned my hair
Upon our wedding morn.

I give it to you
As you leave to-day,
To carry ever next your heart,
My lord.

Guard it well,
To remind you of our love,
And that we are one,
Though a thousand leagues apart.

THE HERMIT

I dwell apart
From the world of men.

I lift my eyes
To the mighty hills,
And sit in silent revery
By rushing streams.
My songs
Are the whisperings of the winds
And the soft murmurs
Of falling rain.

Blossoms open
And flutter to earth again.
Men come
And men go;
Year follows year,
And life goes on.

THE AWAKENING OF SPRING

Lightly, gently, on the city
Falls the warm and welcome rain;
In the bleak and barren courtyard
Springs the soft green grass again.

On the branches, 'mid the blossoms,
Yellow orioles call and swing;
In the bosom of the maiden
Strange desires sing.

THE POOL IN MY GARDEN

In my garden stands an arbor,
In the middle
Of a pool.

On the banks
The reeds grow thick and tall,
With snow-white flowers
In the spring.

Often,
When at night I cannot sleep,
I lie in bed,
And watch the autumn moon
Swim clear and white
In the waters
Of the pool.

A SOLDIER TO HIS WIFE

Farewell!
The hours of birth and death
Are hidden from us;
But, if perchance
I must travel to the Yellow Springs,
My spirit will be at peace,
For I know
That you are ever watching
At the cradle of our son.

A SOLDIER'S WIFE TO HER HUSBAND

If duty to your country means
That you must die
And return to our parent earth
On the far-off north frontier,
Know
That my love for you shall be
As strong and imperishable
As that stone
Upon the mountain side.

[165]

MY SANCTUARY

On the low wall of my garden
There stands a tiny shrine,
Half-hidden
In the shadow of the trees.

When I am weary of this sad world,
And of man's turmoil and strife,
I steal off
To my shrine among the trees.

There, with silent prayer and incense,
I find my soul again—
And thank Heaven
For my shrine among the trees.

THE WANING MOON

Lonely and sad
I stand
Before my door,
And watch the night
Creep on.

The little stream
Flows
Under the bridge,
On its long, long road
To the sea.

Through the weeping-willow trees
I see the yellow sunset
Slowly die,
And the moon rise,
Pale,
In the east.

AUTUMN RAIN

The autumn wind
Sighs
In the yellow grass.
The pines of the forest
Moan,
And the dead leaves
Whisper
At my window.
My feeble lamp
Flickers,
As though it, too,
Must die.

A LETTER FROM HOME

Over three thousand li
Of winding stream
A letter—just a few short lines—
Has come.

Each line repeats the question
Of the last;
Each only asks,
"When are you coming home?"

LOST HAPPINESS

I sit and dream
Of the happy days
When you brought these pearls
For me;
Of the mornings when
I combed my hair,
And you the while
Penciled
My eyebrow's curve.

And to-day?
Ah, to-day I dwell alone;
And you are wandering—where?

I fear to walk in my garden,
Lest I see
A pair of butterflies
Disporting in the sun
Among the flowers.

THE CAPTIVE

A Tartar captive,
Toiling in the sun,
A thousand li
From the land of Han—
What a bitter fate is mine!

Hark! How sweet is that flute
With its reedy note,
And the thoughts that it brings
Of home!

MIDNIGHT

How still and silent
The pavilion in the courtyard
Is at midnight!

The flowers
Stir in their sleep,
And from under the hedge
A solitary cricket calls.

Half in a dream
I hear the whisper of the wind,
And from my bed
I watch the bamboo's slender shadow
Wave across my window
Like a flag.

THE BUDDHIST TO HIS SOUL

This world is but illusion,
Light and shadow;
All desire, void and empty,
Yet ceaseless, without end.

Nirvana itself
Evolved
From darkness into light.

Then dare, my soul,
To drink deeply,
But, being drunk,
Remember
The awakening
That must come.

THE SCHOLAR

The evening wind
Has rolled back
The curtain
Of the clouds.
The moon shines clear,
And the sky is bright
With the gleam
Of distant stars.

Though you
Are far away
From home and me,
I see you
As you always were
At this hour of the night,
In your study,
Poring over
Your loved books.

FISH!

We are yesterday's catch
Being taken to market.
Our eyes are wide open
To all that goes by.

If only we could send word
To our friends in the river
To hide in the deep holes—
For prices are high!

A LAMENT

Five long years
Have come and fled,
Since last
The voice of my dead mother
Spoke.

And still
I sit and mourn
For her.
The bitter tears
Well up
And stain my cheeks.
The joy of life
Is gone.

I cannot even
Bear to see
The mother bird
Feed her nestlings
On the bough.
Ah, me!

NIGHT RAIN

I sit through the long night
In the high tower,
And listen to the autumn rain
Outside my window.

There is no sound of human life,
Save now and then
A belated traveler hastening by.
Through the dark heavens
A wild goose
Wings his lonely flight.
In the chill gloom
A cricket calls.
The water drips mournfully
From the t'ung trees,
And the blossoms
Flutter sadly
To the rain-soaked earth.

Sadness broods
Over the world.

DREAMS

I awoke with a start
In the fifth watch of the night.
My lamp had sunk low,
Had flickered and died.

The vain tears were still flowing
That I had shed in my sleep,
For my dream had brought
Fresh pain to the wounds
In my heart,
To old wounds I had thought
Long healed.

THE FIFTH WATCH OF
THE NIGHT

Look, my love!
The waning moon
Still sheds its fading light.
Do you hear that frightened bird
Calling for the dawn?
How mournful is its cry,
How lonesome for its nest
And mate!
Not yet, my own!
Cling to me,
Close to my heart.
I cannot let you go!

AN OLD GARDEN

The mists of thirty years
Have drifted by
Since I left home.
Pale ghosts, and wraiths
Of long-dead days,
Flit through the garden paths
And vanish like a dream.
A flock of geese
From northern climes
Flies overhead
In the silent, moonlit night.

Oh, for a letter
From that far-off land,
From the home I love so well!

THE COMING OF AUTUMN

All night long
The wind whispers and sighs,
And the rain, in fitful gusts,
Rattles and beats
At my west window.

I toss and turn,
And wake from fitful dreams,
While in the court outside
The dry dead leaves
Join in the drear
Sad autumn dirge.

NIGHT AT YEN CHOU

The fishermen
Are meeting by the stream.
As they move,
Their blazing torches
Cast queer shadows
That dance along the sand.

The far-off trees
Gleam silver
In the half-moon's light.
From a temple,
High in the hills,
Booms out
The call to prayer.

THE FAN

There lies her fan, gold-flecked,
Just as it was that day she gave it,
In remembrance of our love.
Again and again I turn to it,
Unable to avert my eyes
For long.
But she
Whose hand once held it
Has passed
To that eternal round of change
Which even the lowly silkworm
Undergoes.
She too,
Though well beloved,
At her hour foreordained
Passed to the silence
Without end.
Seven long years
Have come and gone since then,
But all the fragrance and enchantment
That were hers
Still linger
In the folds of faded silk.

NOONDAY

I think
I never loved her more than now,
As she lies asleep at noonday
On her couch.

There she is,
Beautiful to behold,
Her fan fallen from her tiny hand,
Her great golden pins
Thrust loosely through her hair.

The yellow lilies
And the pines
Appear to shrink and turn away,
As though fearing
To disturb her blessèd sleep.

While I?—
I gently reach out a stealthy hand,
To span the length
Of her tiny silken shoe.

THE KITE

Shears and paper
Shaped my frame;
A kite am I!
With naught but a child
To guide my way,
I ride the sky!

When wild winds blow,
I leap and dance
In maddest joy!
Oh, all you puny men below,
Look up at me!
A kite am I!

THE POEM OF TEN "ONES"

A flower,
A willow,
A fisherman
On a rock.

A ray of sun
On the river,
A bird
On the wing.

Halfway
Up the mountain
A priest slowly climbs
To a shrine.

In the forest
A yellow leaf
Flutters and falls.

THE BELL IN THE NIGHT

The wick of my lamp
Has sunk and died.
Long have I turned and tossed
On my bed,
But slumber will not come.

The moon creeps softly
Through the courtyard,
Where the flowers are asleep,
And, from a distant hill,
Comes the sweet chime of a temple bell,
Throbbing through the night.

THE MORNING BELL
OF FANG T'A

In the east of the city,
Near my home,
Stands the great, square, stone pagoda.

I lie on my pillow
And hear its chimes
Riding the winds of night.

And when, each morning,
Through my curtain
I see the glow of dawn,
I know not if the world is real,
Or a vision and a dream.

TO MY SISTER

Twelve months ago this morning,
You and I
Were happy with each other
In this house.

Since then, time has moved so slowly
That it seems
As though many, many years
Had passed away.

The idle spring wind blows aside
My screen.
I look into the courtyard
Just outside,
And I am jealous
Of the smiling flowers,
Rejoicing with their sisters
In the sun.

WHICH?

Slowly,
Over the mountains, piercing the haze,
The moonlight breaks
Through the green pine trees.

Its light shines
On a maiden fair,
Under a flowering plum.

Oh, who can say which
The most lovely is,
The maiden, the moon,
Or the flowering plum?

A WIFE TO A HUSBAND

For fifteen years we've never been
A single day apart.
How can I bear to think that now
A score of days—eternity—
Must lie between us two?

Last night I cried myself to sleep,
And in a restless dream
I saw you leave, clung to your arm,
Awoke—and wept again.

FROM EXILE

To-day carries me back
A long, long year.
Again I feel you
Clinging to my sleeve,
And our children
Tugging at my knees
In last farewell.

To-night
I am alone,
Save where,
In the dying lamplight,
Restless shadows
Move and creep,
And in the dreary watches
Of the night
No one ever comes
To talk of home.

FAREWELL TO SPRING

The last pale gleam of spring
Has died away.
In the wind the faded petals
Drift and fall.
I turn to my book for solace,
But in vain.
There are some heartaches and sorrows
Too poignant for a poet
To sing
In his lays.

A FLUTE AT EVENING

The dewdrops cling
To the green bamboos
Like pearls.
The wind stirs lazily
In the lotuses,
And their pale red petals
Flutter to the earth.

As the night creeps on apace,
The twinkling glowworms
Light my path,
And faintly, from a tower
In the east,
Calls a bamboo flute.

GATHERING BAMBOO

Since you have left my side,
My lord,
I have no joy in the jades
That once adorned my hair.
My love for you
Is deep as the waters of Hsiang,
And the tears I shed in loneliness
Have stained the green bamboo.

A BELL AT EVENING

In the distance
The mountains are draped
In cloud.
Through the willows that line
The Ts'in Kuan road
I can see the village huts.
Over the flower-strewn fields
Comes the booming call
Of a temple bell.
The sun has set.

GOOD NEWS

More than a year has passed
Since you and I
Parted in grief and tears.

To-day at last
A letter came,
One tiny, narrow sheet.

To-night I've lit my lamp
A hundred times
To read its words of love.

RAIN AT NIGHT

At eventime I walk beside
The fragrant lotus-pool.
With the twilight comes
A drizzling rain,
And now the willow trees
Have become but darker shadows
Against the darkening sky.

I stand alone
On the tiny bridge,
Alone, in a world of gray,
Save for a single heron,
Flying low,
Through the mists
That veil the stream.

FORLORN

Grasses
Rippling in green waves before the breeze,
Peach blossoms
Tossing red upon the stream,
Spring wind
Wandering out upon the deep—
Which of you
Does not pity me my fate?

THE DRUNKARD

My cart jolts over
The river road,
And the ten li to home
Seem a thousand miles
In the dark.

I'm afraid unto death
That the bright round moon
That's leaping from tree to tree
Will fall from the sky
And knock me down,
And I'll never see home
Again.

A DESERTED GARDEN
ON THE ROAD TO
HUA CHOU

How all is changed with the years!
No one ever comes now
To look upon the beauty
That was here.

The long bridge that spanned the lotus pool
Has fallen into ruins.
In the last rays of the setting sun
Ten thousand lotus buds
Pour forth their fragrance,
And in the old trees
The locusts chirp
Their mournful evensong.

FEVERED SLEEP

I lay sick.
The demons of ill
Held me tightly
In their grasp.
In vain
I tossed upon my pillow,
And sought sleep.
My lamp had sunk low and died
In the watches of the night,
And all was dark.

I saw—
Or did I dream I saw?—
The courtyard,
Half in shadow,
Half in silver,
Where the moon crept up the sky.
Then the flowers came,
And danced—
Or were they only shadows,
That climbed the wall
And peeped in through the window
Where I lay?

THE LAMP AND THE MOON

My silver lamp
Sways gently in the wind,
And the graceful shadows
Dance
Upon the wall.

I draw back my screen,
And see the pale moon,
Shining on a sleeping world.

Through the open window
Drifts the scent of blossoms,
And, from afar,
I hear
The plaintive piping
Of a flute.

RIDING AT DAYBREAK

Not a man is stirring
In the early light,
As my horse trots
Through the rustling yellow leaves.

The pale waning moon
Fades slowly in the dawn,
And a temple bell calls
Through the frosty air.

Far off,
Where forest trees loom through the mist,
A mountain torrent
Rushes down its stony bed.

THE HAPPY FARMER

All the long night
The rain pattered down
On the thick, thatched eaves
Of my hut.

This night, on ten times
Ten thousand farms,
It has stirred the rice seed
To new life.

When the warm sun comes up,
I shoulder my hoe
And go blithely forth
To my field,

And I sing a song as I go,
Of the blue, blue sky,
And the water that shines
So green.

SHADOWS ON THE WALL

The evening mist
Creeps on the world.
From a lonely shrine
Rings out
The sunset call to prayer.
Across the old red wall
Steal slowly
Long, dark-green shadows.

The booming bell
Brings back to me
The place where once
I wrote a song,
Ten long, long years ago,
And again I see
The blossoms fall
Upon the deep green moss.

THE MOTHER

His grandmother
Grieves long
And bitterly
For her grandchild,
Who is dead.

His father
Is worn out,
His eyes red
With weeping
For his son.

But I?
Though my heart breaks
And turns within me,
No tears will come,
Even
When they lift my little child,
To dress him
For his grave.

THE FLUTE

When I had a little leisure,
I gave my son some lessons
On the flute.

Autumn has come,
And in the courtyard
The wei plants
Are flaming red.

On the wind
I hear his piping,
And my heart
Is filled with joy,
That his flute
Can bring such pleasure
To my happy little boy.

THE HOSTESS

My little son
Runs up to me
With gleeful shout
And laugh.
A guest has come!

How shall I receive him?

As good luck
Would have it,
The chrysanthemums
Have opened
Their first buds—
So there's our decoration!
Our home is poor,
Our food is crude;
It may not suit his taste—
But we have
Some fine old wine on hand.
That
Will help us out!

AUTUMN SUNSET

The waters whisper softly
On the shore of Ch'ing Tsao lake.
Over Huang Ling temple
Hang the gray-tinged clouds
Of sunset.
A single boat with widespread sail
Scuds before the fresh west wind,
And in the distance
Winds the mountain road
That leads to Yüeh Yang.

THE FLEETING YEARS

Ten years ago, when I left home,
Yün Ying, young, unmarried,
Was a famous beauty
And the talk of all the town.

To-day we met again.
I asked her married name.
We talked and shared our wine.

From behind the cup
I scanned her face.
Then came home the bitter truth—
That I have become an old, white-haired man.
And I am sorrowful
Unto death!

MEMORIES OF CHILDHOOD

The moon
Casts the shadow of the plum
Upon my bed.

I remember well
That day so long ago
When with these hands
I planted that old plum.

Last night was chill and sharp,
And the cover of my bed
Was scant and thin,
But the fragrance of the plum
Stole through my dreams,
And I forgot old age
And frost and cold.

Awaking, I looked out,
And there the bright moon shone
On the newly opened blossoms
Of the plum.

SEPARATION

Though the river still flows seaward
As before,
And the spring still bubbles
From the mossy ground,
Life has never been the same to me
Since you left home.

Yesterday I climbed the high hill,
And it seemed
As though again I saw
The white sail of your boat,
Fading swiftly in the distance
Like a dream.

WEDDED TO A TARTAR*

My father
Gave me in wedlock
To a chief of the Wu Sun tribe.
I dwell
In a strange wild country
At the far-off end
Of the earth.

My home is a yurt
With walls of felt.
Red meat is my food
And mare's milk my drink.

My heart ever yearns
For the land of my birth.
Ah, that a snow-goose
Would lend me its wings
To bear me back once more!

* An autobiographical poem.

REJECTED

There you flutter
Before our bed,
Stirred by the passing breeze.

I brought you
With me
When I left my home,
To screen our love
From the blinding light
Of day.

With cords
I bind you carefully
And lay you
In my chest,
For today I take you
With me,
Back to my father's house.

I wonder when—if ever—
I shall unroll you, my curtains,
And hang you once again.

HOMELESS

A stranger stood without the gates;
He had travelled ten thousand li.
I asked,
"Who are you?
From what land do you come?"

Sighing, he answered,
And poured forth to me
The story of his heart,
Weeping the while,
Till his sleeve was wet with tears.

"I am a scholar from a northern land.
I have lived in the towns of Ch'ên
And have dwelt in the kingdom of Wu,
But knowing no rest
I wander again
And go forth to the land of Ch'in."

VISITING THE CHOU FAMILY TOMBS

Today
The sun shines brightly,
And the cheery call of crickets
Fills the air.

Though we give some sober thought
To those
Who sleep beneath the trees,
How can we refrain
From present happiness?

As we sing our merry songs
Together
The jade-green wine
Brings smiles and laughter
With its fragrance.

We know not
What tomorrow may conceal,
But for today
All care has vanished
From our hearts.

THE CALL OF SPRING

The blossoms are open
On the cassia tree
And the orchid has unfolded
Its first green leaves.

In vain the happy wind of Spring
Will laugh,
If you do not keep your promise
To return.

A SONG OF PARTING

The mountain tops
Are hidden in white clouds;
The soft breeze
Has ceased its whispers
In the pines.

If you would know
The sorrow in a wanderer's heart,
Gaze on the moon
From the lonely terrace steps.

DOUBT

The waters in the gorge
Flow deep,
And over a thousand li
Is flung
A mantle of pure snow.

My heart is steadfast
As the cedar and the pine,
—But yours?
Ah, how can I know
What place I have therein?

TO AN EARLY PLUM

Awaking early from your winter's sleep
To greet the Spring,
You alone of all the trees
Dread not the cold.
Yet perhaps in truth
You fear to lag behind
The other flowers of the year
Lest men cease
To give you love and praise
Beyond the rest.

ON HEARING A BLACKBIRD AT CH'ANG AN

Here in Ch'ang An,
A foreign town,
Ten thousand li from home,
A blackbird startles me
With its sudden burst of song.

Oh, little blackbird!
I am a stranger here.
Why do you sing to me
Songs of your native land?

THE WILD GEESE

The leaves are falling
By the arbor where you left me,
And the mists are rising
At the parting of the roads.

Alas!
How strange are men!
Why can they not travel
As the wild geese do,
Departing and returning
Altogether,
In a row?

THE SOUTH ARBOR

The shady arbor
Stands apart
In a riot
Of bright flowers.

I am lonely,
For I find no friend
To drink with me.

The Spring wind
Stirs my flowing sleeves
As I sit,
Dreaming beside the stream
—And all the while
The bells boom out
The call to evening prayer.

THE MOUNTAIN COURTYARD

The sharp wind stirs
The countless leaves,
And the autumn air is chill
On the mountain side.

At dawn
The white frost glistens
On the grey-green tiles;
At eve
The westering sun gleams red
Through the bars
Of my lacquered balustrade.

THE SONG OF THE CANDLE

Your flame nods
In the gentle breeze
Like a blossom
Opened ere Spring has come.

You shed a thousand tears,
Yet you have no thought
For the sorrows of mankind.

LUNG MÊN TEMPLE

It is more than a year
Since last I came
To the temple of Lung Mên.

The old priest leads me to a cell—
My lodging for the night.

Who will ever know
The surge and stir within my breast
As I watch the rising
Of the crescent autumn moon,
And listen to the age-old roar
Of the far-off waterfall?

MOURNING FOR LI SAN

Last autumn,
Old friend,
You were here by my side,
Singing "The Waters of Wei."

'Tis Spring.
I stand on the Shang Lo terrace
And weep.

In grief
I raise my voice to Heaven,
To cry out against the injustice
Of your fate.

Why, if you had to die so young,
Did Heaven endow you
With such rich gifts
Of genius,
And why
Have you left behind
A wife on a bed of pain
And a fatherless baby girl?

WHITHER?

Where is there happiness today?
To be sad,
To shed tears,
Are both in vain.

This life is naught
But a dream in the night.
A few short years—
And all is done.

THE WILLOW BY THE RIVER

I planted a willow
On the river bank
At old Chiang Nan.

For two long years
Have I wandered far from home.

Often
I dream of the vivid green
That lines the shore,
And wonder
Who is gathering
The branches of that willow
Beside the river at Chiang Nan.

CARING FOR SILKWORMS

Spring is here again,
And with it wings the wild goose
From the South.

In the dying glow of sunset
I lay aside my work
And sit and idly dream—
Long dreams of you,
Of where you are,
And when you may return.

PARTING IN THE RAIN

The falling rain
Made the pain of parting
Even greater;
My tears themselves
Were as the drops that fell.

My heart rises
To the clouds
And fares a thousand li
Upon the sea
In the hope
That you and I may meet again.

AUTUMN MOON

The new moon
Hangs yellow in the sky,
And the autumn night
Is wet
With heavy dew.

The chill air
Pierces my thin garment,
And I long for my winter's silks.

I have played
Upon my silver lute
The whole night long,
But my heart is sad,
And I dread
Returning
To my empty, dreary room.

TO HIS BROTHER

The long year is at an end,
And the wild soldiers
With their spears
Have laid waste the greatest city
In the land.

I sent a letter
To learn if you still lived,
Or if you, alas, had perished
With the rest.

All unexpected
Came your answer,
As though fallen from the skies.

Ah!
Who can know
The countless tears of joy
My eyes have shed?

FAREWELL TO PO CHÜ I

Why reproach me
Because I linger?
True it is
I only came to say farewell.

But oh, how hard it is
To leave you,
For our hair is white,
And good old friends are few.

Remember, too,
Tomorrow
You may not be as happy
As today!

LONELY OLD AGE

As the years go by
The old familiar faces
Vanish, one by one.

I, old man Sun,
Am about to go,
And my robe
Is wet with tears.

I cannot learn
Before I die
What my journey's end may be,
But I now know
That this old frame
Is very near its final resting-place.

I AM CONTENT WITH LIFE
AND AT PEACE WITH THE WORLD

Today I have wine,
Today I shall sing,
Today I shall drink my fill.

Anger and sorrow
Are but wasted hours.
Let the cares of tomorrow
Wait on tomorrow's sun.

REVERIE

In the old garden
I sit, a stranger,
With none to share my wine.

For whom, then,
Have the pear and the peach
Opened wide their fragrant petals?

The Spring tide
Heeds not
The griefs and woes of men.

See!
With the evening rain
It comes rolling in again
From Hsi Hsing town.

TEMPLES BUILT WITH HANDS

The dwellers
In the old city
Are countless
As the waves of the sea.

A teacher came.
At his behest
They raised a lofty temple,
Pouring out golden treasure
For dreams
Not of this world.

And now
In the Hall of a Thousand Gods
I sit
And watch the incense smoke
Curl up
And vanish
In thin air.

A NIGHT IN SPRING

The night wind comes
In short, sharp gusts.
The incense glows red in the golden bowl,
And the drip, drip,
Of the water-clock
Is stilled.

The beauty of the night
Drives slumber from my eyes,
As I watch the moon-etched shadows
Of the blossoms
Slowly drift across my screen.

IMPROMPTU

Your heart is fickle
As the weed
Upon the stream,
Yesterday
Stirred by the southern wind,
Today
By that from the north.

My heart is firm
As the temple of Ch'i P'ao,
And as unchanging
As the crest of Nan Kao Fêng,
That looks ever to the north
Toward the peak of Pei Kao Fêng.

HOME

I have planted a garden
On the eastern slope.
The grass is lush
And the tendrils of the melons
Have grown long.

It is sunset.
The autumn shadows of the trees
Are chill.
Aimlessly I walk alone,
Meeting no one, save now and then
Some weary peasant,
Resting by the road.

I wander in the twilight
By the stream,
And listen to the temple bell
Calling softly
Through the mist.

I am happy in my garden
And my field;
They bring me full content.

MORNING PRAYER

The long temple banners flutter
In the wind,
And the blue smoke rises
From the glowing incense bowl.

I cling tightly
To my younger sister's arm,
While she supports our mother
As we walk.
Together
We climb the hillside to the shrine
To offer prayer and incense
To our God.

Then slowly we descend the steps
And walk upon the verdant moss
Wet with the dew of early morn.

SPRING RAIN

Though Spring has come
It has rained
The whole day long,
And few people
Pass my door.

From a branch
Of the green wisteria vine
A lazy oriole
Idly calls.

NIGHT REVERIE

I have turned back
My flowing sleeves
And laid aside
My green-stringed lute.
The empty court is eerie,
And I fear to be alone.

In the silence of the night,
Heavy with the fragrance of the tea plants,
I walk among the bamboos
And the flowers.

The River of Heaven*
Glows like a fiery mist,
And my lamp
With its pale green shade
Gleams as a star
Through the open door.

* The Milky Way.

THE PINE TREE

The pine by the road
Is tiny now,
And its blue-green leaves
Tell of its tender years.

Yet in days to come
It will tower to the clouds,
And cast its cooling shadow
On the traveller beneath.

NOTES

Page 112. "A Lament for My Son Ts'ui."

Têng Yu, fleeing from the power of Shih Lo, was robbed of his horses and oxen, and was obliged to continue his flight on foot, carrying his son and his nephew on his back. Finally, feeling that he could not save them both, he tied his own child to a tree and went on with his nephew and his wife, saying to her: "My brother is dead, and, if my nephew were to die, there would be no one to continue my brother's line; but I may have another son."

Page 135. "Eventide."

Yang Kuei Fei, the author of this poem, is famous as the most beautiful woman in all Chinese history. She was a favorite of the Emperor Ming Huang. Her influence over him became so great that his soldiers, mutinous, demanded her death, and by his orders she was strangled.

Page 186. "The Poem of Ten 'Ones'."

In this poem the Chinese character for "one" is used ten times; hence the title.

Page 195. "Gathering Bamboo."

"At the traditional site of Shun's grave to-day there grows a slender speckled bamboo. The people say that the marks upon the bamboo are made by the teardrops of his two wives, who visited his grave and wept together." —E. T. Williams, *A Short History of China*, p. 32.

BIBLIOGRAPHY

Addenda on pp. 256–58

(Exclusive of works in Chinese and Japanese)

Abbreviations: BSOSL—Bulletin of the School of Oriental Studies, London; JNCBRAS—Journal of the North China Branch, Royal Asiatic Society, Shanghai; MSFOS—Mittheilungen des Seminars für orientalische Sprachen, Berlin.

Alexéev, V. M.
  Kitaiskaya poema o poete. (Russian.) Petrograd, 1916
Allen, Clement F. R.
  The Book of Chinese Poetry. London, 1891
Ayscough, Florence
  "Chinese Poetry and Its Connotations," JNCBRAS, LI:99, *Tu Fu.* London, 1929
Ayscough, Florence, and Lowell, Amy
  Fir-Flower Tablets. Boston, 1921
Ball, J. Dyer
  Rhythms and Rhymes in Chinese Climes. Hong Kong, 1907
  Things Chinese. Ed. 5, Shanghai, 1925
Barrow, John
  Travels in China. Ed. 2, London, 1806
Belpaire, Bruno
  Quarante poèmes de Li Tai Pé. Paris, 1921
Bernhardi, Anna
  "Li T'ai Po," MSFOS, XIX:105
  "Tau Jüan-ming," MSFOS, XV:58
Bernhardi, Anna, and von Zach, E.
  "T'ao Yuan-ming," MSFOS, XVII:179
Bethge, Hans
  Die chinesische Flöte. Leipzig, 1926
  Pfirsichblüten. Berlin, 1932
Böhm, Hans
  Lieder aus China. München, 1919

[247]

BROSSET, M.
    Essai sur le Chi-King. Paris, 1828
BUDD, CHARLES
    Chinese Poems. Oxford, 1912
    "Chinese Poems," JNCBRAS, LXI:165
BYNNER, WITTER, AND KIANG KANG-HU
    The Jade Mountain. New York, 1929
CHINI, M.
    Nuvole bianche. Lanciano, 1918
CHRISTY, ARTHUR
    Images in Jade. New York, 1929
CLARK, CYRIL D. LE GROS
    Su Tung P'o. London, 1931
CLEMENTI, SIR CECIL
    Cantonese Love-Songs. Oxford, 1904. 2 vols.
COULING, SAMUEL
    Encyclopaedia Sinica. Shanghai, 1917
COUVREUR, S.
    Cheu King. Ho Kien Fou, 1896
CRANMER-BYNG, L.
    The Book of Odes (Shi King). London, 1920
    A Feast of Lanterns. London, 1916
    A Lute of Jade. New York, 1918
    The Vision of Asia. London, 1932
DAVIS, SIR JOHN
    Poetry of the Chinese. Macao, 1834
    Poetry of the Chinese. New ed., London, 1870
DE HARLEZ, C.
    La Poésie chinoise. Bruxelles, 1892
DE LA GRASSERIE, RAOUL
    Essai de métrique chinoise. Paris, 1893
D'HERVEY SAINT-DENYS, LE MARQUIS
    Poésies de l'époque des Thang. Paris, 1862
    Le Li-Sao. Paris, 1870
DI GIURA, L. N.
    Poesia de Li-Può. Lanciano, 1928

ERKES, EDUARD
  Chinesische Literatur. Breslau, 1922
FLETCHER, W. J. B.
  Gems of Chinese Poetry. Shanghai, 1917
  More Gems of Chinese Poetry. Shanghai, 1919
  "The Song of a Skirt," JNCBRAS, LII:193
  "A Trip to Kua Kang," JNCBRAS, LII:192
FORKE, ALFRED
  Blüthen chinesischer Dichtung. Magdeburg, 1899. 2 vols.
  Dichtungen der T'ang- und Sung-Zeit. Hamburg, 1929. 2 vols.
GAUNT, T.
  Ling Yin Monastery Poem, JNCBRAS, LIII:93
  Little Garden from Cathay. Shanghai, 1919
GAUTHIER, JUDITH
  Le Livre de jade. Paris, 1928
GILES, HERBERT A.
  A Chinese Biographical Dictionary. London, 1898
  Chinese Literature. London, 1901
  Chinese Poetry in English Verse. London, 1898
  Gems of Chinese Literature:Verse. Shanghai, 1923
  Two Chinese Poems. Shanghai, 1873
GRANET, MARCEL
  Festivals and Songs of Ancient China. London, 1932
  Fêtes et chansons anciennes de la Chine. Paris, 1929
GRUBE, WILH.
  Geschichte der chinesischen Litteratur. Leipzig, 1909
HAMMOND, LOUISE STRONG
  "The Tunes of Chinese Poetry," in *Year Book of Oriental Art and Culture, 1924–1925.* London
HART, HENRY H.
  A Chinese Market. Peking, 1931
HAUSER, OTTO
  Die chinesische Dichtung. Berlin, n.d.
HEADLAND, ISAAC TAYLOR
  Chinese Mother Goose Rhymes. New York, 1900
HEILMANN, HANS
  Chinesische Lyrik. München, n.d.

HSIEH PING HSIN
    Spring Water, trans. by GRACE M. BOYNTON. Peking, 1929
HUBRECHT, ALPH.
    Etymologie des caractères chinois. Peking, 1932
HUNDHAUSEN, VINCENZ
    Der Blumengarten von Tang Hsiaen-Dsu. Peking, 1933
    Chinesische Dichter. Peking, 1926
    Gedichte von Tau Yüan Ming. Peking, 1928
IKBAL 'ALI SHAH, SIRDAR
    The Oriental Caravan. London, 1933
IMBAULT-HUART, CAMILLE
    La Poésie chinoise du xivme au xixme siècle. Paris, 1886
    Poésies modernes chinoises. Peking, 1892
    "Poète chinois du xviiime siècle (Yüan Tseu-ts'ai)," JNCBRAS, XIX,
    Pt. II:1
JENNINGS, WILLIAM
    The Chinese Shi King. London, 1891
JOERISSEN, GERTRUDE L.
    The Lost Flute. New York, 1929
JOHNSON, KINCHEN
    Peiping Rhymes, First Series. Peiping, 1932
KARLGREN, BERNHARD
    The Poetical Parts in Lao Tsi. Göteborg, 1932
    Sound and Symbol in Chinese. Oxford, 1923
KLABUND, pseud. (ALFRED HENSCHKE)
    Dumpfe Trommel und berauschtes Gong. Leipzig, n.d.
    Li-Tai-Pe. Berlin, n.d.
KLIENE, CHARLES
    "The Land of Peach Bloom," JNCBRAS, L:108
KOO, T. Z.
    Songs of Cathay. Shanghai, n.d.
    Songs of the People. Shanghai, n.d.
LEGGE, JAMES
    The Book of Poetry. Shanghai, 1931
    The Chinese Classics, Vol. IV, Pts. I and II. Oxford, n.d.
    The Sacred Books of China, Vol. III in *The Sacred Books of the East*,
    ed. by F. Max Müller. Oxford, 1899

LIM BOON KENG
    The Li Sao. Shanghai, 1929

MARTIN, W. A. P.
    The Lore of Cathay. New York, 1912

MAYERS, WILLIAM F.
    The Chinese Readers' Manual. Reissue, Shanghai, 1924

MOULTON, JAMES R.
    The Literary Study of the Bible. Ed. 2, Boston, n.d.

OBATA, SHIGEYOSHI
    Li Po. New York, 1922

OEHLER-HEIMERDINGER, ELISABETH
    Das Frauenherz. Stuttgart, n.d.

PARKER, E. H.
    John Chinaman. London, 1902

PAUTHIER, G.
    "De la poésie chinoise," in *La Revue encyclopédique,* février 1833. Paris

PFIZMAIER, AUGUST
    Elegische Dichtung der Chinesen. Wien, 1887

PLATH, JO.
    Ueber zwei Sammlungen chinesischer Gedichte aus der Dynastie Thang. München, 1869

POUND, EZRA
    Cathay. London, 1915

PURCELL, V. W. W.
    The Spirit of Chinese Poetry. Singapore, 1929

SEUBERT, ADOLF
    Chinesische Gedichte. Leipzig, n.d.

SOONG, TSUNG FAUNG
    La Littérature chinoise contemporaine. Pékin, 1919

SOULIÉ DE MORANT, GEORGE
    Essai sur la littérature chinoise. Paris, 1921
    Florilège des poèmes Song. Paris, 1923
    "Poèmes de lasciveté parfumée," in *Anthologie de l'amour chinois.* Paris, 1932

STENT, GEORGE CARTER
  "Chinese Lyrics," JNCBRAS, VII:93
  Entombed Alive. London, 1878
  The Jade Chaplet. London, 1874
SUNG-NIEN HSU
  Anthologie de la littérature chinoise. Paris, 1933
  "Quelques poèmes de Tou Fou," *Revue franco-chinoise*, XII, Nos. 3 and 4. Paris, 1931
TCHANG, FONG
  Le Paon. Paris, 1924
TCHOU, KIA-KIEN, ET GANDON, ARMAND
  Anthologie de la poésie chinoise. Pékin, 1927
TOUSSAINT, FRANZ
  Le Flûte de jade. Paris, n.d.
TSÊN TSONMING
  Anciens poèmes chinois d'auteurs inconnus. Lyon, 1929
  Essai historique sur la poésie chinoise. Lyon, 1922
  Une Goutte d'eau. Paris, 1925
  Rêve d'une nuit d'hiver. Lyon, 1927
UNDERWOOD, EDNA WORTHLEY, AND CHI HWANG CHU
  Tu Fu. Portland [Maine], 1929
VAN DOREN, MARK
  An Anthology of World Poetry. New York, 1928
VISSIÈRE, A.
  "Quelques mots sur la poésie chinoise," *Revue franco-chinoise*, X, No. 3
VITALE, BARON GUIDO
  Pekinese Rhymes. Peking, 1896
WADDELL, HELEN
  Lyrics from the Chinese. London, 1914
WALEY, ARTHUR
  "Further Poems of Po Chü-i," BSOSL, 1918
  "Hymns to Kuan-Yin," BSOSL, 1920
  More Translations from the Chinese. New York, 1919
  "Notes on Chinese Prosody," *Journal* Royal Asiatic Society, April, 1918
  170 Chinese Poems. New York, 1919
  Poems from the Chinese. London, n.d.
  Poet Li Po (The China Society Lectures). London, 1918

WALEY, ARTHUR *(concluded)*
    "Pre-T'ang Poetry," BSOSL, 1917
    The Temple. New York, n.d.
    "Thirty-eight Poems by Po Chü-i," BSOSL, 1917
WATTERS, T.
    Essays on the Chinese Language. Shanghai, 1889
    "Life and Works of Han Yü, or Han Wên Kung," JNCBRAS, VII:165
WERNER, E. T. C.
    Chinese Ditties. Tientsin, 1922
    Chinese Sociology. London, 1910
    A Dictionary of Chinese Mythology. Shanghai, 1932
    Myths and Legends of China. New York, 1922
WHITALL, JAMES
    Chinese Lyrics. New York, 1923
WHYMANT, A. NEVILLE J.
    "Chinese Coolie Songs," BSOSL, 1920
WIEGER, LÉON
    Caractères chinois. Ed. 4, Hsien Hsien, 1924
    Chinese Characters. English ed., Hsien Hsien, 1927
WILDER, J. D., AND INGRAM, J. H.
    Analysis of Chinese Characters. Peking, 1921
WILHELM, RICHARD
    Chinesisch-deutsche Jahres- und Tageszeiten. Jena, 1922
    Die chinesische Literatur. Potsdam, 1926
WILLIAMS, E. T.
    China Yesterday and To-day. Ed. 5, New York, 1932
WILLIAMS, S. WELLS
    The Middle Kingdom. Revised ed., New York, 1913
WOITSCH, L.
    Aus den Gedichten Po Chü-i. Leipzig, 1916
    Lieder eines chinesischen Dichters und Trinkers (Po Chü-i). Leipzig,
    1925
WYLIE, ALEXANDER
    Notes on Chinese Literature. Reissue, Shanghai, 1922
ZOTTOLI, ANGELO
    Cursus litteraturae Sinicae neo-missionariis accomodatus, Vol. V. Shang-
    hai, 1882

(CHINESE AND JAPANESE WORKS CONSULTED)

中文書目

中國詩史

白話文學史

詩的作法

中國八大詩人

詩體釋例

古今詩選

中國白話詩選

歷代女子詩選

歷代名媛詩

中國歷代女名家詩選

歷朝香奩詩

五百家經詩

詩經

古詩源

全漢三國晉南北朝詩

玉臺新詠

沈歸愚古詩源

欽定全唐詩

唐詩三百首

御定全唐詩

白香山詩集

白話詩話居歴詩

王詩

宋詩

五絕百首

詩集詩鈔

明宋石坡詩鈔

元話安東坡詩代朝朝園朝眞烈鶴雪雲香華晚安雲

宋白王蘇東元近本國隨國長徐雲咏小韻瑤楚雅倚

詩集詩鈔選閣子州集詩館詩集詩屋詩

詩詩詩詩鈔詩存草

鈔鈔選錄鈔

集詞

詩詞

日文書目

漢和詳唐校

詩漢解詩註

入名詩名選唐

門詩類新選

評釋

選選

ADDENDA TO BIBLIOGRAPHY

ANON.
>   *Distinguished Men of the T'ang Dynasty.* (Chinese & Japanese Repository)

ACTON, HAROLD, AND CH'EN SHIH-HSIANG
>   *Modern Chinese Poetry.* London, 1942

AYSCOUGH, FLORENCE
>   *Travels of a Chinese Poet.* London, 1934

BYNNER, WITTER, AND KIANG KANG-HU
>   "A Poem of the Stone Drums (Han Yü)," *China Review.* New York, 1920

CANDLIN, CLARA M.
>   *The Herald Wind.* London, 1933

CHENG CHI-YU
>   *New China in Verse.* Berkeley, 1944

CH'U, T. K.
>   *Chinese Lyrics.* Cambridge, 1937

CHUNG PARK LUM
>   *Chinese Verse.* New York, 1927

CLARK, CYRIL LE GROS
>   *The Prose Poetry of Su Tung-Po.* Hong Kong, 1935

COLVIN, IAN
>   *After the Chinese.* London, 1927

CRANMER-BYNG, L.
>   *The Never-Ending Wrong.* London, 1902.

EITEL, E. J.
>   "The Shee King," a review of Legge's translation. *Chinese Recorder.*

FAN CHÊNG-TA
>   *The Golden Year.* Cambridge, 1946

FORKE, ALFRED
>   *"Einige Verse des Wang Wei,"* Ostasiatische Zeitschrift, II

FRANKE, O.
Kêng Tschi Tu. Hamburg, 1913

GILES, HERBERT A., AND WALEY, ARTHUR
Select Chinese Verses. Shanghai, 1934

HART, HENRY H.
The Hundred Names. Berkeley, 1933
A Garden of Peonies. Stanford, 1938
The West Chamber. Stanford, 1936

HOFFMANN, ALFRED
Frühlingsblüten und Herbstmond. Köln, 1951

HU SHIH
"The Social Message in Chinese Poetry," *Chinese Social & Political Science Review,* VII

HUNG, WILLIAM
Tu Fu. Harvard, 1952

JENYNS, SOAME
Selections from the Three Hundred Poems of the T'ang Dynasty. New York, 1940.
A Further Selection from the Three Hundred Poems of the T'ang Dynasty. New York, 1944

KURZ, HEINRICH
Das Blumenblatt. St. Gallen, 1836

LARIOS, JUAN RUIZ DE
Antología de la Poesía China. Barcelona, n.d.

LIN YUTANG
The Gay Genius (Su Tung Po). New York, 1947

LUH, C. W.
On Chinese Poetry. Peiping, 1935

MANENT, MARIA
L'Aire Daurat. Barcelona, 1946

MEDHURST, W. H.
"Chinese Poetry," *China Review,* IV

PAYNE, ROBERT, ed.
Contemporary Chinese Poetry. London, 1947
The White Pony. New York, 1947

TIETJENS, EUNICE, ed.
> *Poetry of the Orient.* New York, 1928

TREVELYAN, R. C., ed.
> *From the Chinese.* Oxford, 1945

VISSIÈRE, A.
> "*Les Herbes* (Po Chü I)," *Bull. de l'Assoc. Amicale Fr.-Chin.,* I
> "*Le Poète* Tou Fou," *Bull. de l'Assoc. Amer.-Fr.-Chin.,* I

WALEY, ARTHUR
> *Chinese Poems.* London, 1946
> *The Life and Times of Po Chü I.* London, 1949
> *The Poetry and Career of Li Po.* London, 1950

WANG CHING-WEI
> *Poems.* London, 1938

WIMSATT, GENEVIEVE
> *Selling Wilted Peonies.* New York, 1936

INDEX OF AUTHORS

INDEX OF TITLES